Henri Pène du Bois

Four Private Libraries of New York

A contribution to the history of bibliophilism in America. First series

Henri Pène du Bois

Four Private Libraries of New York
A contribution to the history of bibliophilism in America. First series

ISBN/EAN: 9783337418953

Printed in Europe, USA, Canada, Australia, Japan

Cover: Foto ©ninafisch / pixelio.de

More available books at **www.hansebooks.com**

HENRI PÈNE DU BOIS

Four Private Libraries of New-York

A CONTRIBUTION TO THE HISTORY OF
BIBLIOPHILISM IN AMERICA

First Series

PREFACE BY OCTAVE UZANNE

NEW-YORK
DUPRAT & CO.
1892

Copyright, 1891, by DUPRAT & Co.

TO
OCTAVE UZANNE,
PARIS:

𝕲𝖗𝖆𝖙𝖎𝖙𝖚𝖉𝖊—𝕬𝖋𝖋𝖊𝖈𝖙𝖎𝖔𝖓.

HENRI PÈNE DU BOIS,
NEW-YORK.

PREFACE BY OCTAVE UZANNE.

Paris, le 26 Octobre, 1891.

*M. Henri Pène du Bois,
New-York.
Vous voulez bien, cher Monsieur, m'annoncer votre prochaine publication, "Quatre Bibliothèques Particulières de New-York," qui doit servir, par la suite, à l'Histoire de la Bibliophilie en Amérique.
Vous ajoutez qu'il vous serait agréable de publier quelques lignes de moi en tête de ce "Livre d'Or" des <u>amoureux du livre</u> aux États-Unis, et je me rends aussitôt à votre invitation, d'autant plus volontiers que je suis en quelque sorte le parrain de cet ouvrage, dans l'ancien <u>Livre</u> où vous eûtes accès comme rédacteur correspondant pendant plusieurs années : je ne saurais l'oublier.
C'est, sans aucun doute, en mémoire de ce parrainage qu'il vous convient de me demander si je veux bien agréer la dédicace de ce livre curieux, et c'est également en souvenir de nos*

bonnes relations qu'il me plaît d'accepter cet hommage lointain.

J'ai grand désir curieux de lire votre étude, principalement parcequ'elle traite de quatre célèbres cabinets new-yorkais dont les "bibliothèques merveilleuses" hantent souvent les conversations des amateurs de Paris avisés sur la bibliophilie du Nouveau Monde.

Parmi ces amateurs d'outre-atlantique, dont vous allez être le bibliographe, deux font partie de la Société des "Bibliophiles Contemporains" et, à ce titre, déjà ils me sont chers; deux autres sont membres du "Grolier Club" . . . <u>et amicorum</u>, c'est-à-dire qu'ils détiennent chez eux des reliures aux ors éclatants signées par Derome, Le Gascon, Roger Payne, Matthews, Marius-Michel et autres "ensoleilleurs de maroquins."

Comment voulez-vous que je ne m'intéresse pas à de tels Mécènes des beaux livres, lorsque je crois savoir que l'un d'eux est M. Jolly-Bavoillot, un des plus fervents bibliognostes du globe, qui jadis, en de longues lettres ardentes et spirituelles, me faisait communier avec ses enthousiasmes; quand je perçois qu'un autre répond à la caractéristique bibliophilesque de M. George Beach de Forest dont j'ai ouï dire merveille et que les <u>Biblio-Contempo</u> sont heureux de compter dans leur sein.

Votre livre, cher Monsieur, sera apprécié par tous les français dilettantes de livres, car la bibliophilie possède une langue universelle qui défie tous les volapuck du monde, et qui ne réclame aucun interprète.

Il sera, j'en suis assuré, fort bien accueilli à Paris, aussi bien qu'à Londres, et nos bons amis les Russes, même, ne seront pas insensibles à l'éloquence des beautés décrites par vous.

Si je n'étais rivé à mes constants labeurs sur les quais de la Seine, et s'il m'était donné de saisir le loisir de quelques semaines nécessaires pour passer au pays du "Grolier Club," j'aimerais vous avoir pour cicerone dans ses mirifiques librairies dont vous vous êtes fait l'annonciateur.

Je suis sûr qu'à New-York, parmi vous, je me sentirais dans une intimité amicale, douce et pénétrante, car la passion du livre unit tous ceux qui en sont atteints, et il ne peut y avoir ni gêne ni froideur lorsque les mains palpitent sur de nobles maroquins et qu'une admiration mutuelle extasie à la fois le possesseur et son hôte.

Les relations, du reste, deviennent chaque jour plus cordiales entre bibliophiles d'Amérique et de France ; bientôt, grâce aux sociétés, aux revues spéciales, aux visites, et aux fréquents échanges d'idées, l'entente sera parfaite et l'on devra aux livres qu'il n'y ait plus d'océan.

Il y en a un toutefois à cette heure, et je dois à cet infini aquatique de n'avoir pu lire votre ouvrage <u>fût-ce en épreuves</u>, afin d'avoir le plaisir de le préfacer.

Il m'eut été agréable d'y placer une ouverture de ma façon, en connaissance de matière. Laissez moi, cependant, faute de ne pouvoir mieux faire, souhaiter à vos quatre <u>monobibliographies</u> un succès continental, et croyez, cher Monsieur, à mon amicale confraternité et à l'expression de mes sentiments de haute bibliomanie sympathique.

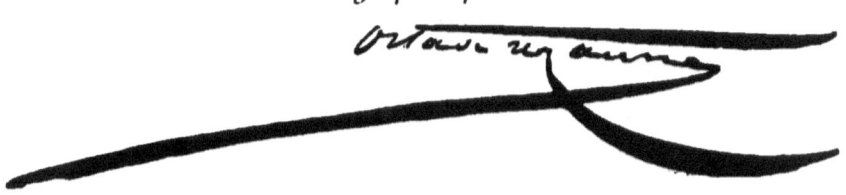

LIST OF CHAPTERS.

	PAGE
Preface by Octave Uzanne	5
The Art of the Decade	15
Library of the Romanticists	19
The Work in Detail	23
Alfred de Vigny	34
The Art of Bookbinding	37
Historical Book-Covers	42
Books of To-Day	54
The Elzevirs	73
The Vignettists	84
Original Illustrations	92
A Blue Diamond	103
A Book of Thackeray	108
An Epic of Pierrot	113

LIST OF ILLUSTRATIONS.

PAGE

BINDING IN MOSAIC, BY TRAUTZ-BAUZONNET . FRONTISPIECE
EX-LIBRIS C. JOLLY-BAVOILLOT, BY GIACOMELLI . . . 19
BINDING IN MOSAIC, BY CUZIN 23
FACSIMILE OF LETTER OF VICTOR HUGO 30
BINDING MADE FOR GROLIER 46
BINDING BY WILLIAM MATTHEWS 62
ORIGINAL ILLUSTRATION BY GEORGE H. BOUGHTON TO
"KNICKERBOCKER'S HISTORY OF NEW-YORK" . . 66
BINDING INLAID WITH LILY OF SILVER, BY RUBAN . . . 80
EX-LIBRIS GEORGE B. DE FOREST, BY PAUL AVRIL . . 84
BINDING BY COBDEN-SANDERSON 100
ORIGINAL ILLUSTRATION BY VAN MUYDEN TO BRILLAT-
SAVARIN'S "PHYSIOLOGIE DU GOÛT" . . . 104
BINDING IN MOSAIC, BY MONNIER 110
BINDING IN MOSAIC, BY DE SAMBLANCX-WECKESSER . . 112

FOUR PRIVATE LIBRARIES
OF NEW-YORK

"𝔥ere begynneth the folys and
firste of inprofytable bokys."

BARCLAY.

THE ART OF THE DECADE.

The art of forming a library was divined at the time when the French unlearned the poetic art codified by Boileau. At that time Didot wrote to Lamartine:

"I have read your verses. They are not without talent, but they are without learning. They resemble nothing received and required from our poets. One does not know where you have taken the language, the ideas, the figures, of this poetry. It cannot be classified with any definite style; it is a pity, for there is harmony in your verses. Renounce these novelties which would denationalize the genius of France; read our masters Delille, Parny, Michaud, Raynouard, Luce de Lancival, Fontanes. These are the poets cherished by the public; resemble somebody if you wish to be recognized and read! I would be a bad counselor if I encouraged you to publish this volume, and I would be serving you badly by publishing it at my expense."

The volume was the "Méditations Poétiques"; it was printed in 1820, a few weeks after Didot's letter, and at Didot's printing-house if not at his expense. Less than twenty years later the Didot dynasty knew that its literary authority had vanished. Lamartine, Hugo, Gautier, Vigny, Musset, luckier than Louis-Philippe, governed. They had not imitated Delille and the rest that the public liked; on the contrary, they had written masterpieces which the public hates. Instead of making money, they had made the art of France the most recent expression of the beautiful. And the Didots, undone in literature, fell with all the weight of their antique Philistinism on the art of the printer, illustrator, and book-binder, on the art of forming a library. They fell as tyrants on an unguarded citadel. It would take volumes to relate this lamentable history.

They printed the poets of the seventeenth and eighteenth centuries who were not poets. They spoiled thus all the good paper that there was in Holland, and left to the artists the paper of the greengrocers. They exalted, in reports of public exhibitions where they were judges more implacable than Æacus and Rhadamanthus, Simier above Thouvenin, the pseudo-classics, the worn-out ideas of book-making, the faded ideals of book-collecting. In their autocracy they were aided by the men who were forming libraries. These obeyed because in obeying they needed not to think or work or be artists. For fifty years of artistic liberty a library was formed with less application than a laborer gives to the breaking of stones on the highway. There was a Draconian rule. Anybody who had money and a manual obtained missals, incunabula, books with wood-engravings, books with vignettes, books from famous libraries; and to give them the most recent expression of the beautiful marked them with an insignificant book-plate.

Canevari, Maïoli, Grolier, De Thou, Hoym, Spencer, Nodier, Didot, Brunet, Brinley, collected books like coins.

They were indifferent to the latent life of them. As they obtained them they let them remain. Not a book of their libraries derived an advantage from having been in their possession. They bound them, but their bindings were their impersonally elegant marks of possession, uniform, invariable, inexpressive of the books that they covered. They described them, but their descriptions fitted editions. THEY DID NOT KNOW THE ART OF BOOKBINDING. THEY WERE NOT LOVERS OF BOOKS; perhaps they were lovers of bibliomania. They have in the art of forming a library the place in the art of poetry occupied by Delille, Parny, Michaud, Raynouard, Luce de Lancival, Delavigne, and Ponsard, that abolished pleiad. There was one book-lover who understood this in the time of their exaltation by the Didots. He divined the art of forming a library because his mind, with regard to book-collecting as practised by others, was blank as a white page. It had not been affected by false ideas. It was the mind of Charles Asselineau, the mind of a poet, faithful to Ronsard's eloquent admonition in the "Abrégé de l'Art Poétique Français," "You must have, in the first place, conceptions elevated, grand, beautiful, and not trailing on the ground."

Asselineau was a Romanticist partial to the verge of injustice. The literary and artistic revolution of 1830, a Renaissance not less beautiful than that of the sixteenth century, naturally evoked many men like him. They were fanatics; others, in their view, were atheists. Asselineau was deaf and blind to a humanity antedating 1830 and not extinct in 1840. He knew intimately every celebrated Romanticist of that great epoch. He admired even those who had been celebrated for an hour, and not more than an hour: Louis Bertrand, Ernest Fouinet, Félix Arvers, Regnier-Destourbet, Eusèbe de Salles,

Napol le Pyrénéen, Emile Cabanon, Théodore Guiard, Philothée O'Neddy, Théophile de Ferrières. But Victor Hugo's "Légende des Siècles," published many years after 1840, was "a posthumous work" of the great poet! This explanation of Asselineau in defense of his chronology was a vertiginous trope, but not more surprising than the one in the "Poésies de Joseph Delorme" of Sainte-Beuve, which he took literally and drew with pen and ink:

> Pour trois ans seulement, oh! que je puisse avoir
> Sur ma table un lait pur, dans mon lit un œil noir.

Aglaüs Bouvenne made a facsimile of the drawing, which was a precious relic of the Asselineau library—a library of works of the Romanticists, "lavés, encollés," filled with scarce vignettes, portraits, and autographs, bound by Capé, Bradel, or Lortic; a library every volume of which was unique in a novel sense: a volume of the printer and bookbinder made a volume of the artistic book-lover. That such a work was possible astounds; but what will you say of the Titan who demonstrates that it may be surpassed by fidelity to the art of the decade!

For the art of the decade does not ask of one to make a chronology of the Romanticists which shall begin in 1830 and end in 1840. It does not ask of one to collect books of the Romanticists. It is more exacting. It requires that a collection of Romanticists, or of Historical Book-Covers, or of Elzevirs, or of Vignettists of the Eighteenth Century, or of Masterpieces of Literature, shall be perfect in its smallest details.

LIBRARY OF THE ROMANTICISTS.

THE work of the Titan is in a room small enough to dance, with its three cases of mahogany and large desk, the grand galop of the Bal Musard in the least vast of the rococo library-rooms.

The shelves admit a double row of books, but they are not full; and the desk is for the books that are useful, but there is nothing useful. Asselineau is incorrect, Noilly a trifler, and the others are as ignorant of the bibliography of Romanticism in France as we are of the language of birds before we have read the divine Aristophanes or the tales told in the pictures of Giacomelli.

Giacomelli is the artist of the workman's symbolical bookplate. Clearly the sparrow, gamin of the boulevards, perched above the open book, with a defiant, mocking air, adds "Surpasser" to the legend inscribed on the page. To "Aimer, Admirer" the sparrow adds the third element of the art of forming a library. To loving and admiring it adds surpassing that involves universal knowledge. It means that, to form a library, one will never know too well history, philosophy, the theologies, esthetics, the fine arts, the sumptuary and decorative arts, and all the languages. Logically, for the library formed is a poem in the strict Greek sense, a composition the expression of which is absolute, perfect, and definitive.

Thus is the library of the Romanticists of France. It was formed by Mr. C. Jolly; it is his work as much as the "Légende des Siècles" is Hugo's, and it is like a poem because the least change or alteration would diminish its beauty and exactitude. It is the only library of the Romanticists ever formed, and, while it exists, it will be almost as difficult to form a library of poetry and a library of literature as for a cable to pass through the eye of a needle.

"Why do not you say that it will be quite as difficult? If it contains poems of Hugo that are not elsewhere, the library of the Romanticists must render impossible the formation of a library of poetry!" the Philistine will not fail to remark. The objection is absurd and frivolous! The formation of a library is a work of genius, and genius always finds the occasional causes of its creations, since these creations must happen. The same workman shapes genius and chance, and shapes them for each other.

What better illustration of this may be given than the formation of the library of the Romanticists? Their literature was exactly the reverse of the literature of to-day. It was independent. The most laborious writer could not dispose of more than two novels in a year, and he sold them for a few hundred francs; but these books were his life, his imagination of a poet, all his conceptions and all his dreams. To-day the public pays and consequently commands. The publisher has the right to say: "This style of love," or "this style of assassination," "does not please my customers." In the time of the Romanticists the public had no voice in the matter because it bought no books. There was nothing to prevent a poet from writing "Notre Dame de Paris" or "Mademoiselle de Maupin" when he wished and how he wished, if he had the ability. But the sale of his works never exceeded six hundred copies. When there were six hundred and fifty copies of a work by Balzac sold, his friends asked anxiously : " What is the matter? Has he made dishonest concessions? " At present, when three months after the publication of the book the new novelist has not sold his twenty-thousandth volume, his friends are alarmed, and they ask : " Is he failing?" For his masterpieces Hugo was insulted like a criminal by people who supposed that they were attacking only his glory. If he had not been a giant, he would have died of hunger. Of his unsold books of poems in extravagant editions of three hundred copies, the shopkeepers made wrapping-paper. What, pray, were the chances of obtaining intact volumes of the Romanticists ten or twenty years ago?

Conquet made the chances fainter. That intrepid little man could not but make his way in the world. He is a famous publisher; but when he was called, derisively, "l'homme aux couvertures," he was a dealer in old books in a shop, large as one's hand, of the Boulevard Bonne-Nouvelle. He said that a book of the Romanticists was imperfect if it lacked the paper covers wherein it originally appeared. He advertised for paper covers in the "Bibliographie de la France"; he searched the workshops of the bookbinders, the lumber-rooms of the retired greengrocers, and the great collections of the provincial landlords. His rival, Rouquette,— a Gascon and a *roublard*, Rouquette! — was the first to announce a book of the Romanticists for sale, with the original paper covers. It was a work of Barthélemy, and it is recorded in the Rouquette catalogue of December, 1876.

All the books of the Library of the Romanticists have their original paper covers. They are typical, they are documentary, they are often works of art. They make an accessory bibliography of books which have not appeared. On the back of Petrus Borel's " Rhapsodies," Paris, 1832, is this list of promised publications :

Pâture à Liseurs, Petrus Borel.
Appel aux Jeunes Français à Cœur de Lion, Petrus Borel.
Odelettes, Gérard.
Mosaïques, Philadelphe O'Neddy.
Odes Artistiques, Théophile Gautier.
Mater Dolorosa, Augustus MacKeat.
Essai sur l'Incommodité des Commodes, Jules Vabre.

Not one of these books ever saw the light of day ; but the last of the list is famous, and has famously noted its author. Jules Vabre is the author of a book which was never written. He is the author of nothing else.

"MOSAÏQUE," PROSPER MÉRIMÉE.
BINDING IN MOSAIC BY CUZIN.

THE WORK IN DETAIL.

The books of the library of the Romanticists are all first editions, uncut, with the original paper covers, bound by an artist, faultless, explained with notes, ornamented with scarce illustrations, illuminated with autograph letters and verses of the authors. The library has everything, and everything perfect: the pure curiosities, as "Louisa, ou les Douleurs d'Une Fille de Joie," 1830, by the Abbé Tiberge (Regnier-Destourbet); the "Contes de Samuel Bach," 1836, by Théophile de Ferrières; and "Un Roman pour les Cuisinières," 1834, by Emile Cabanon; the collections of "Contes Bruns," 1832, and "Annales Romantiques," 1823-36, and the prospectus wherein Jules Janin designated as "Quentin du Roi" (Regis) the celebrated novel of Sir Walter Scott; the unsuspected original issues of works of Hugo, Lamartine, Musset, Sainte-Beuve, Quinet, Gautier, Vigny, Barthélemy, Méry, Dumas, Janin, Glatigny, Banville, Sand; and of all the illustrations of Deveria, Johannot, Daumier, and Célestin Nanteuil; and of their critics, censors, and parodists.

There are "Feu et Flamme," 1833, by Philothée — sometimes Philadelphe — O'Neddy, in real life Théophile Dondey, with a dedicatory epistle; "Les Roueries de Trialph," 1833, of Lassailly, with marginal notes in manuscript of Vigny; the "Myosotis" of Hégésippe Moreau, with this manuscript note, about the book, by Monselet: "Tudieu! quel luxe pour un poète qui couchait sous les ponts"; "L'Idole" of Albert Mérat, with the two suppressed sonnets, "Le Sonnet des Cuisses" and "Le Dernier Sonnet," in manuscript of the author; the "Vignes Folles" of Glatigny, with this quatrain in manuscript of Glatigny:

> Poète dont le feu trop loin du ciel s'allume,
> A mon ami Hardy, j'ai donné ce volume,
> Lorsque chez l'Odéon, le public s'embêtait
> A voir la Karoly déclamer Belmontet.

Poor Glatigny, who was a comedian, studied the art of rhyming, remembered that he was a poet, wrote the language that Gautier and Banville knew, lived on rays of sunlight, returned to the commonplace, and died!

Lamartine wrote a poem to an unknown admirer, "A Un Inconnu." In the "Recueillements Poétiques," 1839, only the second stanza was published, with the title, "A Un Anonyme." The Library of the Romanticists has the poem in the handwriting of Lamartine. This is the first stanza:

> Il est doux pour celui que le génie inspire
> D'entendre son écho vibrer dans plus d'un cœur,
> Des amis inconnus s'attachent à sa lyre,
> Et quand le souffle saint de son front se retire,
> La gloire devient son bonheur.

Sainte-Beuve has written, "Lamartine ignorant, qui ne sait que son âme." Alas! Lamartine did not know even that, but to fall in ecstasy before concerts of angels and repeat the delicious and formidable echo of them, he needed not to know anything.

In "Antony," 1831, are these verses in the handwriting of Alexandre Dumas:

Que cherches-tu sur notre terre étrange,
Esprit du ciel perdu dans nos chemins ;
Ne crains-tu pas de blesser tes pieds d'ange
Aux durs cailloux de nos sentiers humains ;
Ne crains-tu pas qu'un parfum ne dévoile
Ton origine à ceux qui te verront,
Ou que le vent qui soulève ton voile
Ne fasse luire une étoile à ton front ?

In "Emaux et Camées," 1858, is this line in the handwriting of the impeccable poet Théophile Gautier, whose country was that of the Hellenes, the country of temples, white statues, and forests visited by gods, and who liked the clearness, the joy, and the healthy irony of France:

Je suis satisfait de cet exemplaire et je le signe pour en augmenter l'éclat. Théophile Gautier.

In the "Stalactites," 1846, of Théodore de Banville, who was an exile from Heaven, and, fearing to forget its language, learned no other, are these verses in his handwriting, similar to the handwriting which one attributes to the fairy Titania:

Que les temps sont changés ! * mon cher Asselineau ;
Pour moi l'enfant Amour allumait son fourneau,
Lorsqu'en des lieux charmants, remplis de clématites,
Je rêvais ce recueil nommé les Stalactites,
Tout jeune encore, ainsi que Damète ou Tircis.
Hélas, c'était en mil huit cent quarante six,
Epoque où j'étais cher à la Grâce indécente,
Et j'écris ces vers en mil huit cent soixante,
N'ayant presque plus d'or et d'argent sur le front,
Vieux lyrique fourbu, dont les jeunes riront !

* Racine, "Athalie."

In Alphonse Karr's "Sous les Tilleuls," 1832, is the wide white ribbon, embroidered in blue with the name of Alphonse Karr on one side and Nice on the other, which the Olympian Jupiter of the sages sent gracefully with every bunch of roses of his garden. There are the inexcusable "Livre d'Amour," 1843, which Sainte-Beuve supposed he had completely destroyed, but nothing is ever destroyed; the most romantic love-story of the century in "Elle et Lui," "Lui et Elle," and "Lui," the story of George Sand and Alfred de Musset, told by George Sand, Paul de Musset, and Louise Colet—Louise Colet who was a Nereid of Rubens, and to whom solid Romantic faith gave, in a statue named " Penserosa," the figure of a dreamy young woman. There are the eight octavo volumes of Alfred de Musset — "que personne ne posséda et ne possédera jamais," said Asselineau—and the "Nouvelles" of Alfred and Paul de Musset, extended by the insertion of a "Nouvelle" of Alfred, "Les Frères Van Bruck," not to be found in any edition of his works, but specially reprinted for this volume from the *Constitutionnel;* "L'Anglais Mangeur d'Opium," 1828, and the copy of De Quincey's work, the identical copy which Alfred de Musset used for his work of adaptation, and not translation, as the publisher supposed; the fourteen volumes of plays, three volumes of which are for "Le Chandelier," altered for the stage; and an infinity of original notes and letters of the poet to his brother and to his friend Alfred Tattet about his poems, his tales, and his plays. There is Musset in the exquisite lithograph made by Gavarni; Musset, proud, charming, young, and handsome as he appeared at an evening reception at Nodier's, when he read the "Contes d'Espagne et d'Italie," 1830, and instantly was famous; Musset in the admirable medallion of David, and in several sketches of artists who knew and appreciated him at every stage of his career. In the "Histoire du Roi de Bohême et de Ses Sept Châteaux," 1830, of Charles Nodier, is the lithograph of an evening party "à l'Arsenal," in the apartment of the Bibliothèque de l'Arsenal, wherein Nodier received and charmed the Paris that charmed the world.

There is ALL HUGO.

In the " Recueil de l'Académie des Jeux Floraux" for the years 1819, 1820, and 1821 are the first issues of the " Ode Sur le Rétablissement de la Statue de Henri IV.," which obtained the Lily of Gold premium; "Les Vierges de Verdun," which obtained a special Amaranth premium; "Les Derniers Bardes"; "Moïse sur le Nil," which obtained a special Amaranth premium and the title of Maître ès Jeux Floraux for its author; "Le Jeune Banni," afterward entitled "Elégie"; "Les Deux Ages"; and "Quiberon." The *Journal de la Librairie* made, September 25, 1819, the first public announcement of a work by Hugo. The work was "Les Destins de la Vendée," 1819. The same year appeared, in reply to criticisms, "Le Télégraphe," a satire, and the preface by François de Neufchâteau to the Didot edition of "Gil Blas"— Hugo furnished the notes; in 1820, "Ode Sur la Mort de S. A. R. Charles-Ferdinand d'Artois, Duc de Berry, Prince de France," "Ode sur la Naissance de S. A. R. le Duc de Bordeaux," "Le Génie, Ode à M. le Vicomte de Chateaubriand," and the last of the publications begun in 1819 with Abel Hugo under the title of "Le Conservateur Littéraire," forming three octavo volumes. In 1821 appeared "Ode sur le Baptême de S. A. R. . . . Duc de Bordeaux"; in 1822, "Buonaparte"; in 1823 and 1824, a sequel to the "Conservateur Littéraire," entitled "La Muse Française"; in

1825, "Le Sacre de Charles X.," octavo, and "Le Sacre de Charles X.," quarto, "Par Ordre du Roi"; in 1827, "La Colonne de la Place Vendôme," octavo, and the same duodecimo. In 1830, "L'Aumône," from the cover of which one learns this interesting fact: "Comité de Bienfaisance de Canteleu. . . . Se vend au profit des pauvres. Prix, 1 franc. A Rouen, Février, 1830." At this date it is well to quote the first verses, written on his copy-book as a school-boy, by the creator of French lyrical poetry, in 1815 — that is, fifteen years before "Hernani":

>Ami lecteur, en lisant cet écrit,
>N'exerce pas sur moi ta satirique rage
>Et que la faiblesse de l'âge
>Excuse celle de l'esprit!

In the above LIST were not given the issues of 1822, "Odes et Poésies Diverses"; 1823, second edition, and two editions of "Han d'Islande" in four volumes; 1824, "Nouvelles Odes"; 1826, "Odes et Ballades"; 1826, "Bug-Jargal," two editions; 1827, collective edition of the "Odes" in three volumes; 1828, "Cromwell," and first octavo edition of "Odes et Ballades"; 1829, "Les Orientales," octavo, and the same duodecimo, "Les Occidentales," and "Le Dernier Jour d'un Condamné"; 1830, "Hernani." They were not given in the LIST because they were ever indispensable to a library which pretended to contain Hugo. The LIST is of books of Hugo unknown or indifferent to the old-fashioned collections, indispensable to a library formed in the art of the decade. There are first editions which are proofs before letter, artist's proofs, trial proofs, unfinished proofs, in the libraries of the decade!

In 1832 Renduel published a large octavo edition of the novels of Hugo in this artificial order: Vol. I., "Le Dernier Jour d'un Condamné"; Vol. II., "Bug-Jargal"; Vols. III., IV., and V., "Notre Dame de Paris"; Vols. VI. and VII., "Han d'Islande." Célestin Nanteuil made an etching for each work, but, following the natural chronological order, made of the etching for "Han d'Islande," the first novel, a portrait in a frame of vignettes of Victor Hugo. The edition was published without the etchings; the etchings were never issued. The library of the Romanticists has the four impressions taken by the artist of his work, a masterpiece of this century.

In "Notre Dame de Paris," 1831, is this ex-dono:

A M. Jolly-Bavoillot
Victor Hugo.

There are nominally four octavo editions, 1831, in two volumes, of "Notre Dame de Paris." There was only one impression, divided by fictitious designations on the title-pages, in reality. Conventionally, the first edition is the one not designated. The second edition is the duodecimo edition, in four volumes, published the same year. This is made flagrant by the Library of the Romanticists; the facility for comparison lacking, the evidence is not accessible elsewhere. There is a vignette for the title-page of every duodecimo volume; thus, the duodecimo edition has two vignettes more than the octavo. There is an error on page 71 of the octavo, repeated in the duodecimo; but an erratum after the preface of the duodecimo corrects the error unnoticed in the octavo. The editions, made by mere designations on the title-pages of one impression of the duodecimo edition, are seven in number according to Asselineau, and three in number according to Parran. They are neither seven in number nor three in number: they are two. The first duodecimo edition was numbered fifth, following the fictitious fourth of the octavo; the fictitious second duodecimo edition was numbered sixth; the other, published in 1832, was numbered seventh. There were nominally three editions of the duodecimo, but the second only—numbered sixth—was a fictitious designation. The edition numbered seventh is not a fictitious third edition. It is in reality a second duodecimo edition, revised and corrected, having neither erratum nor error, and containing 306 and 314 pages instead of 322 and 338, as in the first and fictitious second—fictitious fifth and sixth—editions.

In the first edition of "Hernani," 1830,—the second is not fictitious, but a revised and corrected edition,—is this autograph note to Dumas:

Merci, cher Dumas, de votre mot doux et bon. Le jour où vous applaudissiez fraternellement Hernani, j'écrivais pour Maximilien. Ce qui était aussi de la fraternité. *Homo erat.* Aimons-nous. Cher compagnon de luttes, grand et glorieux combattant, je vous serre dans mes bras. Victor Hugo.

In "L'Année Terrible," 1872, is inserted the bard's original proclamation "Aux Allemands," which was posted on the walls of Paris after the siege, and said: "Il me convient d'être avec les peuples qui meurent, je vous plains d'être avec les rois qui tuent."

In "L'Art d'Etre Grand-Père," 1877, is a pen-and-ink drawing of Hugo for his daughter, Léopoldine, labeled in his handwriting: "Abbeville, 4 h. du soir. Dessiné pour ma Didine pendant qu'on attelait la voiture."

H. H. 15 juillet

Merci, cher Dumas,
de votre mot jeune et
bon.
Le jour où vous applau-
direz fraternellement Hernani
j'écrivais par Maximilien.
Ce que était aussi de la fra-
ternité. Homo erat.
Aimons-nous.
cher compagnon de luttes,
grand et glorieux combattant,
je vous serre dans mes bras.

Victor H.

of one impression of the duodecimo edition, are seven in
number according to Asselineau, and three in number ac-
cordin
three i
was n
octavo
bered
seventl
decimo
titious
fictitio
edition
error, :
338, as
sixth —

In t
not fic
autogr

Merc
vous a
Maxim
Aimons
combat

In "
proclar
walls
d'être
avec le

In '
drawin

his handwriting : " Abbeville, 4 h. du soir. Dessiné pour ma Didine pendant qu'on attelait la voiture."

In "Napoléon le Petit," 1852, is inserted the poster, dated London, May 30, 1848, wherein Louis Napoléon Bonaparte appealed for votes at the head of a list of candidates which included "Victor Hugo, Homme de Lettres." In "Les Châtiments" is the poster for the first Republican elections to the National Assembly, containing the names of Louis Napoléon Bonaparte and Victor Hugo as candidates on the same list.

The first edition of the "Châtiments" is not the one that the booksellers regard as the first. The first appeared in Brussels, a 16mo published by Henri Samuel et Cie., in 1853. The preface begins with this phrase: "Le faux serment est un crime," and finishes with this phrase: " Rien ne dompte la conscience de l'homme, car la conscience de l'homme c'est la pensée de Dieu." Proper nouns were suppressed, and in the address "Au Peuple" fifty-six dotted lines replaced a text too bold for Belgian diplomacy. The edition regarded as the first was printed in Jersey the same year, at the Imprimerie Universelle of Saint-Hélier. It is a 32mo, having for places of publication " Genève et New-York," containing an integral text and the same preface as the first edition with this phrase prefixed: "Il a été publié, à Bruxelles, une édition tronquée de ce livre, précédée des lignes que voici," and these phrases affixed: " Les quelques lignes qu'on vient de lire, préface d'un livre mutilé, contenaient l'engagement de publier le livre complet. Cet engagement, nous le tenons aujourd'hui." A counterfeit of this edition has 330 pages instead of 392, and announces, on the paper cover, books which appeared in 1861 to 1868. There were twenty-two copies—sixteen on vellum paper of Holland, and six on China paper—of another edition published. The title-page is: "Victor Hugo. Châtiments [in red ink]. MDCCCLIII. En France." There is no name of printer or publisher. There are two poems added, "Le Christ au Vatican" and "La Voix de Guernsey," the former preceded by this announcement of the publisher : "L'attribution de la pièce ' Le Christ au Vatican' au citoyen Victor Hugo nous a toujours semblée et nous semble encore, aujourd'hui fort douteuse. Cependant depuis plusieurs années cette pièce circule et se réimprime sous le nom du grand poète sans protestation de sa part, à notre connaissance du moins." The protest came in the final edition of the "Châtiments," published by Hetzel— the edition, not dated, where appeared for the first time " Au Moment de Rentrer en France," dated August 31, 1870. In the preface the publisher condemns the counterfeiters and the publishers of "Le Christ au Vatican " and other rhapsodies unworthy of Hugo. But "La Voix de Guernsey" is undeniably by Hugo. The original is a 32mo of sixteen pages, dated Hauteville House, November, 1867, printed on onionskin paper without name of printer or publisher, and entitled, " La Voix de Guernsey. Victor Hugo à Garibaldi." Hugo addressed it to his friends in sealed envelopes like a letter. Every copy detected in the French post-office was confiscated and destroyed. An edition of it was published in Brussels in 1867.

In a great number of autograph letters of the Library of the Romanticists is revealed a Hugo simple, kind, unaffected as a king or a backwoodsman. There is all Hugo expressed : the poet, Hugo-Dante, Hugo-Virgil, young, grave, passionate lover of nature, sad, savage, crowned with the epic laurel of the victorious ; the man, calm in the consciousness of duty done, serene in the consciousness of the prodigious realized, a man of wit superior to all others. There are defined all the Romanticists: possessed by love of poetry, adoration for the beautiful, aspiration toward genius, they reconstructed France. Their works wear ermine, purple, and laurel in an Olympus of books.

ALFRED DE VIGNY.

T HÉODORE DE BANVILLE said that Vigny wore in his features, pure as those of a Greek of the time of Pericles, the distinction which every poet has in his soul. He was a visible sign of the nobility of poets. He had been an officer of the royal guard, his wife was the daughter of a king, and when he threw his mantle of a Count on the emaciated body of Chatterton, the Philistines could not find in him the slightest pretext for their irony. The artist of "Héléna," 1822 "Eloa," 1824; "Cinq-Mars," 1826; "Chatterton" and "Servitude et Grandeurs Militaires," 1835, transfigured Gringoire, Villon, the traditional famished, highway poets, into princes in the train of kings. Is it not a great privilege to be enabled to publish for the first time a tale that he has composed? It is, in the form of a letter addressed to a lady, a document of the library of the Romanticists.

CONTE ARABE.

IL y avait une fois, dans l'Orient du côté de la Mecque, un palais de marbre rose où personne n'osait pénétrer parcequ'il était habité par des génies, à ce que disent les contes arabes que j'ai lus autrefois. Toutes les nuits on voyait des lumières éblouissantes qui illuminaient tout l'interieur de ce grand palais, et les hautes colonnes, les trèfles, les fenêtres longues, les spirales transparentes des escaliers, les cent petits dômes et leurs toits à clochettes, et les pointes des petites tourelles de porcelaine se détachaient en noir sur la lueur égale qui éclairait le palais tout entier. Cependant on n'y voyait jamais l'ombre de personne.

Homme ni femme n'y paraissait, et les lueurs qui s'allumaient tout d'un coup au coucher du soleil s'éteignaient toutes ensemble à son lever.

Quoique toutes les portes fussent ouvertes, il ne s'était trouvé personne, depuis cent ans, qui eût osé les passer, lorsqu'un fidèle croyant qui venait de faire ses dévotions à la Mecque s'aventura jusqu'à une longue avenue de palmiers qui le conduisit aux grandes portes de cèdre sculpté du palais enchanté. Il portait en bandoulière sa petite giberne du Coran sur laquelle il posa sa main gauche, et, tenant son chapelet dans les doigts de sa main droite appuyée sur la garde de son yatagan, il entra d'un pas paisible, en laissant ses babouches rouges sur le seuil de la porte, par respect pour les génies, et ne gardant que ses chaussures de maroquin jaune, il marcha avec confiance sur les tapis très moëlleux, dans de longues galeries, entre deux haies de paravents d'ivoire transparent dentelé et sculpté, qui représentaient les aventures divines de Brahma, et les transformations de tous les génies de l'Orient.

On n'entendait pas le moindre bruit, et le jeune Musulman avait déjà passé à travers quarante-neuf grandes salles désertes, magnifiques, et illuminées, lorsqu'il entendit un léger soupir, et il vit au milieu de la cinquantième salle dorée un trône de marbre noir sur lequel était assise une jeune femme d'une grande beauté.

Après s'être agenouillé devant elle, il fut très surpris de voir qu'elle lui tendait la main, l'attirait à elle et lui donnait un baiser sur le front. " C'était vous que j'attendais depuis cent ans," dit cette jeune femme," et je vous dois le récit de ma vie." Elle le fit asseoir auprès d'elle, et après lui avoir raconté avec un esprit incomparable de grâce et d'éclat, pourquoi les génies l'avaient ainsi condamnée à demeurer seule durant tant d'années, elle l'assura que malgré la magnificence de son beau palais elle commençait à trouver son séjour un peu long, et ne serait point fâchée d'aller ailleurs.

“Eh bien, que ne venez-vous donc avec moi?” lui dit le Mahométan, “puisqu'il était écrit sur le collier d'or invisible que je porte au col, comme tous les vrais croyants, que je devais entrer ici et vous faire voir celui que vous attendiez, il doit être écrit aussi que je vous emmènerai vivre et mourir avec moi.”

“Je ne demanderai pas mieux que de partir sur-le-champ avec vous,” dit-elle, “parceque vous m'avez écoutée toute la nuit, sans m'interrompre et sans montrer d'impatience, et parceque j'ai vu dans vos yeux des rayons et une larme . . . mais voici quelque chose qui m'empêche de partir.”

En disant cela elle ouvrit sa robe de gaze brodée d'or et il vit clairement qu'elle avait les deux jambes et les deux pieds changés en marbre blanc.

J'ai pensé souvent depuis cinquante-neuf jours que ce serait un grand bonheur pour moi, Madame, que d'aller vous revoir et vous remercier de la bonne grâce que vous avez mise à vous informer si souvent de ma blessure, mais j'ai aussi pensé bien souvent que j'avais les mêmes raisons d'immobilité que cette femme enchantée, et j'éprouve, comme elle, le poids d'un pied de marbre que l'on ne peut même pas traîner comme un boulet. Je vous prie donc, Madame, de dire un peu pour moi votre chapelet, et de croire qu'à cette condition je serai bientôt guéri, et en état de vous aller dire combien je vous suis parfaitement dévoué.

THE ART OF BOOKBINDING.

The art of bookbinding is the art of creating in the reader, by the composition of the covers of a book, the state of mind desired by the author of the book.

It is an art of the book-lover, not of the printer, publisher, bookbinder, or author. It is to express the sentiment of the author as it is viewed by the book-lover.

There are two categories of artists: artists who in their work efface themselves, artists who in their work tell themselves. There are book-lovers flagrant and there are book-lovers latent in the books of libraries formed in the art of the decade.

The composition of the covers of a book may engage the plastic arts, all the fine arts, all the arts of decoration. It had not that liberty ten years ago. Then, a Procrustean rule, resting on nothing and having for its object nothing, limited to leather, to MOROCCO LEATHER, to LEVANT MOROCCO LEATHER, and to tiny tools of brass the artistic materials of the bookbinder. Certainly the Italians who worked for Grolier, the Frenchmen who worked for Diane de Poitiers, the Eves, Le Gascon, Padeloup, Trautz, and Lortic, with these materials produced works that are superb, that are magnificent; and they are to be precious examples of handicraft as long as men shall retain the divine faculty of admiration. But these works are examples of decoration with brass tools on leather; they are not examples of the art of bookbinding. They are separable from the books which they cover. Tear them from missals and fit them to tales or to blank leaves, and they will have the same value. They are as inexpressive as tragedies of Luce de Lancival, and for the same reasons. Luce de Lancival knew a hundred words and a thousand rules; the book-lovers of the day before yesterday knew one book and formed collections of ten thousand volumes. In 1830, in the time of the Romanticists, when Homer, Æschylus, Dante, Shakespeare, Michael Angelo, and Mozart in the past, and Hugo and Delacroix in the present, were revered as gods, an idea of the art of bookbinding naturally flashed in the mind of Charles Nodier. Nodier gave it to Thouvenin, and Thouvenin's work shows that he understood it, but he died in poverty in 1834, the only bookbinder with an idea of the entire Romanticist epoch. Firmin Didot was the Aristarchus of the bookbinding exhibitions. At the Bibliothèque Nationale, in Didot's Report for the year 1844, appears the name of a bookbinder who deserves an epic poem. He had the heroism to exhibit a volume on the edges of which an artist had painted a picture, visible when the edges were shown slantwise. He appears, in the Report, summoned to receive a reproof in comparison with which the judgments of Torquemada were sonnets of praise. Perhaps he died of it, for he never appeared again. His name shall be written here in large letters, as a mark of appreciation, for the book-lovers of the decade: BAILLY.

The book-lover is the artist in bookbinding. He does not read, but he has read, his books. He knows them perfectly. The covers that he composes for them shall prove this or prove that he is not a book-lover. I implore the reader to forget any different notion of the art of forming a library which he may have acquired elsewhere. The manuals are made for public libraries or for booksellers, and the books like those of Dibdin, written for book-collectors of an epoch when there were no book-lovers, are not now authoritative. EVERY BOOK THAT PASSES INTO THE LIBRARY OF A BOOK-LOVER OF THE DECADE GAINS AN AUREOLE. It was one of a great number of books lauded or criticized adversely; it was of a limited or of an unlimited edition; its cost was nothing or a fortune; it was literature or pure journalism; its author was unknown or crowned with wreaths of laurel — it is the book of a book-lover. It may be objected that this discrimination has been made in favor of antedecade books of book-collectors, ever since Brunet paid a fabulous price for the "Télémaque" of Longepierre; that at a recent sale the "Libro del Cortegiano del Conte Baldesar Castiglione" brought $900 for no other reason than that it was bound for Grolier; and that "de provenance illustre" is a common note of commendation in the French catalogues. The objection may be emphasized by the fact that the Longepierre "Télémaque" is of the year 1717 edition, and by the fact that the "Cortegiano" was water-stained, and lacked the sixth leaf containing the Aldine anchor. And still it is not a serious objection to the credit claimed for the book-lover of the decade. Books of kings and queens, too, are valuable for their covers marked with arms and devices, but they are not valued as books of booklovers. They are not books, but examples of bookbinding made by artists in decoration, not in bookbinding, for illustrious personages. The "Cortegiano" of Grolier might have lacked a dozen leaves without detriment to its value as a relic of the patron of arts from whom the first club of book-collectors ever formed in America takes its name. But a line lacking in the book of a book-lover of the decade is something inconceivable — as inconceivable as a "Cortegiano" in a library of the decade bound as inexpressively as the "Cortegiano" of Grolier. For all books that are alive are modern, and it does not in the least matter if we lend to ancient authors ideas and intentions which are ideas and intentions of to-day; it does not in the least matter if our interpretation transcends their thoughts. We have the right, and we may regard that right as a duty, to prefer a cover of the decade rather than a cover of the fifteenth century for the "Virgil" of Spira, even if that cover of the fifteenth century was inspired by a psychologist as subtle as Stendhal or by an antiquarian who was also a psychologist. There is nothing alive not modern — and the "Virgil" of Spira, printed in 1470, and the "Cortegiano," printed in 1528, are of the age of Swinburne.

The qualities of the expression in the art of bookbinding are *musical*. The art is to create impressions and evoke images, but by means more complicated and mysterious than the mere representation in conventional or realistic figures of them. It is not by the color of the leather or by a lyre copied at the music-shop that a book of poems may be made expressive in its covers. It is not by copying all the leaves of a tree that the idea of a tree may be communicated to anybody. The covers of a book well bound are decorated in conformity with the subject of the book, the tone adopted, the effect desired, richly or gracefully, gaily or with tragic severity. Formerly a book was well bound in levant morocco with a Grolieresque or Le Gasconesque pattern. It was as if an edict decreed that a woman shall be well dressed in blue or green velvet. She is well dressed in silk, velvet, damask, stuffs with pompadour flowers, or lily-white lawn, according to the scene wherein she appears, drawing-room, opera, park, or library-room. Thus is a book.

HISTORICAL BOOK-COVERS.

W<small>HEN</small> books were dressed in uniformity, like soldiers, they fell in files according to height against the walls of a room, and they filled the space between the floor and the ceiling. In the library formed by Mr. Samuel P. Avery there are rugs of Asia, paintings of masters, bronzes of Barye, vases of King-Te-Tchin, faïence of Deck, and books. The woodwork is ebonized. It forms an arch of balusters infinitely graceful; frames a fireplace; shapes cabinets for prints, books, and bric-à-brac, and above them panels for medallions in bronze, by David d'Angers, of Humboldt, Delaroche, Guizot, Nodier, Johannot, and many other men of science, letters, and art. On the cabinets are the lions and tigers of Barye, the vases in single colors of all shapes and eras; above them are oil-paintings, water-colors, sketches in sepia, works of Madrazo, Vibert, Meissonier. The mantel is surmounted by a mirror, formerly in the house of Boughton, framed in gold and panels representing, in the tall, lithe women that Boughton paints so charmingly, Vanity and Modesty. In the fireplace are bronze andirons made on models of Barye; above it are enamels of Limoges, painted by F. de Courcy, vivid portraits of Benjamin Franklin and Francis Bacon. The ceiling, painted by Galland, with the figure of the genius of painting and her accessories, is as if an archangel had violently torn a panel of azure and revealed a corner of Paradise. There is a glass-covered cabinet filled with books in covers of iron, silver, gold, velvet, and ivory; there are panels of Monticelli, antique stuffs, etchings of Lalanne, Flameng, and Jacquemart, tiny essays signed Detaille. Sifted through windows of stained glass, wherein are traced portraits of Holbein, Correggio, Dante, Shakespeare, Botticelli, Raphael, Dürer, Michael Angelo, their Lauras and Beatrices, the light enchants.

The books are notes in the gamut of plastic and decorative art. There are the book-covers that the Orient inspired to the Italians, figured like the tracings of a Persian manuscript, varnished and wearing the arms of a doge and the lion of St. Mark. There are those that Maïoli liked : in brown calf, inlaid with strips of various colors and ornaments shaped like shells at the center, for the "Roland Furieux," 1552, of Ariosto ; in red, green, and brown calf, for a breviary ; in brown, white, black, and olive, for a book of poems ; divided into four compartments repeating the same design of arabesques in different colors, yellow, black, and green on backgrounds of gold and silver colors, for a volume of 1575 — brilliant, sumptuous, painted once and painted then forever.

There are on a "Historia di Bolognia," 1541, and plates of du Cerceau, 1550, covers of brown morocco, in the center of which is embossed an oval medallion, in gold, silver, and colors, representing Apollo in his sun-chariot driving over waves toward Pegasus. The legend ΟΡΘΩΣ ΚΑΙ ΜΗ ΛΟΞΙΩΣ surrounds the picture. It is the mark of Demetrio Canevari, born at Genoa in 1559, deceased in Rome in 1625, chief physician of Maffeo Barberini of Florence, who became Pope Urban VIII. in 1623. Canevari wrote five learned books about disease and medicine. He formed a collection of valuable books so vast, covered with leather and an ornament so costly, that it absorbed his great gains and made him pass for a miser.

There are covers of white kid, with interlaced initials ҴD, crescents, quiver and arrows, fleurs-de-lis and arabesques inlayed in black with silver outlines, on a book of Charles Estienne, "La Dissertation des Parties du Corps Humain," 1546: a book of Diane de Poitiers, which wears on its title-page the handwriting of the great advocate Le Camus, the handwriting of the Colbertine librarian Baluze, and on the reverse of the front cover the initial and legend, "Inter folia fructus," of Colbert's book-plate. The book appeared as No. 3382 in the catalogue of the Colbert library, published in three 12mo volumes in 1728, with this laconic indication: "L'Anatomie de Charles Estienne, trad. par Estienne de la Rivière. Par. Colinæus, 1546." The auction-sale catalogue of the books gathered by Colbert contained 18,219 titles recommended to the illustrious minister of Louis XIV. by his brother-in-law Charron de Ménars, by his friends Dupuy, Bignon, and Naudé, librarian of the Mazarine library. The Colbert books were bequeathed to his son Marquis de Seignelay, by Seignelay to Archbishop Colbert, and by the latter to Léonore Colbert, Countess Seignelay, for whose benefit they were sold by auction in May, 1728. There was not a more valuable book among them than this book of Diane de Poitiers, emblematic of her, wearing her symbols, the initial of her lover King Henri II., and dressed in black and white, as she was dressed ever after the death of her husband. It is not valuable only as a relic of her, but as a monument of the Renaissance undeniably French. While Catherine of Medici employed foreign artists, and at Fontainebleau French and Italians quarreled and fought like heroes of the Iliad, at Diane's castle of Anet there were no workmen not French, and the men who made her book-covers were artisans as able as if not abler than those of Grolier. The designs on the books of Diane are unmistakably French.

The Grolier design is an imitation of the Maïoli, but rendered in gilt, with an art of gilding that remains until the present time a secret of France. If Grolier's workmen were Italians, they were not more skilful than those of Diane de Poitiers, who were French. If the men who gilded Grolier's books were Italians, they never practised their art in Italy. The device of Maïoli, "Maïoli et Amicorum," which Grolier imitated, was a favorite device of Italian artists in France during the period of the Renaissance, and Jean Cousin, who hated Italian artists, added "et amicorum" to his Latinized name. I infer that the device of Grolier, as the device of Cousin, was a reply of French artists to a challenge of Italian artists. "Io. Grolierii et Amicorum" surpassed "Maïoli et Amicorum" book-covers, as paintings and statues of Jean Cousin and his friends surpassed paintings and statues of the Italian master and his friends. This interpretation is so clear, so evident, that it has no chance of obtaining the favor of those who praise as calisthenics for the mind the art of disputing about nothing. They will continue to say, with Fertiault, Le Roux de Lincy, and many others, that "Io. Grolierii et Amicorum" signified, "This book is for John Grolier and his friends," without an afterthought. They will continue to say this and to ask themselves and others whether or not the device was sincere, for a book-collector whose books belonged also to his friends, even indirectly, even in a purely sentimental, ideal fashion, could not be a book-collector for a longer time than a week. Grolier did not lend his books. His device was not inspired by the book; there was an art of book-covers, and the device meant that it was an art of France. There are in the library of Mr. Avery the covers of brown calf, ornamented with the geometrical design formed of intersecting lines of gold that were Grolier's ideal pattern, made for Alexander Benedetti's "Physici Anatomice Sive Historia Corporis Humani," 1527, No. 35 of Le Roux de Lincy's list. The "Anthropologia" of Galeazzo di Capella, white, in covers ungilt, unmarked with the Grolier marks, has marginal notes in the text and the device, at the end of the last leaf, which appears on the covers of the Benedetti book, written by the hand of Grolier. May this be a sign that I am mistaken in my interpretation of the device, and was it a device applied to books and not book-covers? No; for the covers of the "Anthropologia," white, ungilt, unmarked with the Grolier marks, are Grolieresque nevertheless. They are molded on the book, they have the daintiness, the gracefulness of boards, curved and converging at the edges, of the book-covers of Grolier. In the "Anthropologia" Mr. Avery has a book with trial covers, proofs of book-covers of Grolier. Underestimated is the forwarding, because too persistently praised is the finishing, of a Grolier book. The forwarding is perfectly graceful, and, unlike the finishing, it is inimitable. To verify this assertion, there are one hundred and thirty artisans of book-covers represented in the library of Mr. Avery.

There are the covers, in brown morocco ornamented with a Grolieresque pattern having in the center a lion passant holding a fleur-de-lis, and marked with Roman initials I.R., made for King James I. John Gibson in Edinburgh, and John Norton and Robert Barker in London, were the bookbinders of James I. The Grolieresque pattern came into fashion in England in the time of Edward VI. The book is the "Geographia" of Strabo, 1562-1565, and was No. 2270 of the Beckford-Hamilton Palace auction-sale catalogue. It is a precious example of ancient British handicraft.

BINDING IN CALF-SKIN, MADE FOR GROLIER

There are the conventional sixteenth-century covers of brown morocco, gilded in compartments, made for the "Emblemata et Aliquot Nummi Antiqui Operis," containing plates of the Sambucus collection, a part of the work which is dedicated to Grolier. The book is of the third, 1569, edition; wears on the fly-leaf the arms of the Chifflet family, and on the title-page the signature "Laurentii Chiffletii, 1569," and a presentation of the book to Claude Menestrier, signed Jean Jacques Chifflet. Claude Menestrier was an antiquarian and numismatist, the author of a history of Lyons, the city where lived Grolier. Jean Jacques Chifflet was physician to Philip IV. of Spain, a man of learning famous in all Europe, and the author of twenty-five books, one of which decides the place of Cæsar's first landing in England. Another demonstrated, with a great variety of documents, that the bee was the emblem of the first dynasty of French kings. The bee was the original fleur-de-lis.

There are, on a book of verses of Pindar, 1620, the covers of red morocco, ornamented with fleurs-de-lis and initial letter H in gilt, made for Henri, Prince de Condé. A little book of Herodianus, in mottled calf, with the signature, on a leaf, of J. A. De Thou, is placed in a box made of covers of a book of De Thou. The first edition, Aldus, 1503, of the tragedies of Euripides is in covers of olive morocco covered with gold tooling in the style of Grolier, has the mark of the Lyons library, and comes of an auction sale of the learned Italian Libri, who pilfered many precious manuscripts from French libraries. A "Discorso" of Sebastiano Erizzo, 1559, is in covers of leather chiseled in delicate, ungilt ornamentation, with arms of Fenis du Tournoudel in the center. The "Pithânon Diatribæ Duæ" of Berterius, 1608, is in covers of red morocco ornamented by Clovis Eve with arabesques, leaves, lines straight and curved forming compartments, and in the center the daisy, emblem of Marguerite de Valois, to whom the book is dedicated. A "Historiale Description de l'Afrique," 1556, is in covers of calf with the complicated interlacing of gilt lines favored by the bookbinders of Plantin.

There are the covers of claret-colored velvet, embroidered with fleurs-de-lis, initial M surmounted by a crown and coat of arms of Marie de Médicis, on the "Euphème des Français," 1615, of Jean de Loyac. There are the arms of Jean Jacques Charron, Marquis de Ménars, on a Book of Hours, in vellum, which was numbered 4 on page 405 of the Ménarsiana auction-sale catalogue. The sale occurred in 1718. It began June 10; it finished June 28. Charron saved from a public sale which would have been disastrous the printed books of the library of De Thou. The manuscripts had been purchased for the Colbert library; they are now in the Bibliothèque Nationale; but the printed books were neglected. Charron bought them as they were on their way to a hurried sale, and Santeuil praised his action in a Latin poem of two hundred verses. The printed books of the De Thou library were in the possession of Charron until 1706, when they were overpraised by Germain Brice. Then Charron sold them to Cardinal Armand Gaston de Rohan-Soubise for 40,000 livres, and they were in the Rohan Palace until the Revolution.

The "Calate Fantastiche che Canta Naspo Bizaro," 1565, is in covers of red morocco with the arms of the Doge Foscarini, once librarian of Saint Mark and compiler of the "Lettatura Veneziana." The "Austrasiæ Reges et Duces Epigrammati, Per Nicolaum Clementem Trelaum Mozellanum

Descripti," 1591, is in covers of calf gilt with the mark of Charles I. when Prince of Wales. The book was a duplicate of the British Museum, sold by auction in 1787, a dark epoch when historical book-covers had not the value that they have since attained. The "Œuvres Diverses" of Fontenelle, 1728, are in covers of red morocco with the arms of Mme. de Pompadour, by Derome or Padeloup. In the catalogue of her library, published by Hérisson in 1765, this work is No. 2271. Mme. de Pompadour had eight thousand books, only two of which, the "Roman de la Rose" and "Le Roy Modus et la Royne Ratio," were manuscripts. Her books were classics, and prove that Latour, the great pastelist, who represented her at a table loaded with works of the philosophers, did not paint for her grave surroundings that he imagined.

There is a "Nouveau Testament," 1672, in covers of gold, and wood delicately carved, of the Holy Land, for the Duchesse de Longueville. A miniature prayer-book of 1673 is in filigree of silver, and has at each corner a heart of porcelain painted with the figure of a saint. Psalms of 1637 are in covers of needlework embroidered with tulips. A Bible of 1650 is in wired embroidery of a vase and flowers, with ornaments of silver, by the nuns of Little Gedding. A German note-book is in boards of wood covered with morocco, embossed with a copperplate of Justice in the center of one cover and of Love on the other. A communion-book has clasps formed of crucifixes in silver gilt. A German Bible of Leyden, 1599, is embroidered with a figure of the woman of Samaria on one cover, and of the Virgin and Child on the other. A holiday book, "Etrennes Mignones," of 1780, is in covers of needlework, white, with colored wreath, crown, leaves, and spangles.

"In Funere Carol. III. Hispaniar Regis," Parma, 1789, is in velvet covers purple-colored, ornamented with coat of arms, embroidered in silver and gilt, and bordered with medallions of metal representing antique subjects. An "Almanac Généalogique," 1783, is in covers of white silk, embroidered with crown, drum, trumpets, flags, a soldier with a halberd, and the initial L of King Louis XVI.

There are two books in covers of scarlet morocco with arms of Marie Leczinska, queen of Louis XV. The work of binding is by Padeloup. One of the books is a "Semaine Sainte," prayers for Holy Week; the other is a "Répertoire Dramatique," 1775, a catalogue of selected plays of the Comédie Française. The latter is filled with notes and additions in the handwriting of Louis XVI.: the little, careful, easily legible calligraphy of a personage who made locks, clocks, furniture, notes about actors and their parts, with the irritating, scrupulous accuracy of one compelled; and was king of France, perhaps because the wildest fancy of a poet must be realized, and Racine invented a century before the Revolution this surprising association of words: "Un prince déplorable." The books of Marie Leczinska were sold by auction at the hall of the Archives in Paris in 1849; the "Répertoire Dramatique" was bought by Jules Janin, and was No. 509 of the catalogue of his library.

There are covers of olive morocco, paneled with gilt lines, and ornamented at the corners of the panel with flowers and dots gilt, made by Roger Payne for the "Matthæi de Cracovia Tractatus," printed by Gutenberg in 1460, in the type of the "Catholicon." There are covers of olive morocco made by Mackenzie for the "Series of Ancient Baptismal Fonts," 1828, of Francis Simpson, Jr., containing the India proofs and etchings, which were limited to twenty-five copies, and the original illustrations of Simpson. The book comes of the Hamilton Palace library auction sale. There are the covers of red morocco with border of green, the green above the red, made for "The Contrast: a Comedy in Five Acts, by a Citizen of the United States," 1790, "the first play represented by a regular company on the American stage written by an American writer," to wit, Royal Tyler. It was the book of George Washington, and has his familiar autograph on the title-page.

There is, in covers of blue morocco with blind tooling by Bedford, Bishop Thomas Watson's "Holsome and Catholyke Doctryne," 1558, marked with the signatures of William Stanley, 1673, and Robert Southey, Bristol, 1802. William Stanley was Prebendary of St. Paul's in 1684, Canon Residentiary in 1689, Archdeacon of London in 1692, and Dean of St. Asaph in 1706. In 1802 Southey, then in his twenty-eighth year, was the celebrated author of "Joan of Arc," and he was ardently cultivating the quality which made of him, in the view of Byron, "the only existing man of letters in England." He was collecting facts innumerable about orders Cistercian, Franciscan, and Dominican. The book-stall keepers of London, Paris, Madrid, and Lisbon knew him well. He praised Verbeyst of Brussels : " Think ill of our fathers which are in the Row, think ill of Colburn, think ill of the whole race of bibliopoles, except Verbeyst, who is always to be thought of with liking and respect." When Verbeyst announced the shipment of a parcel to him, "le roi n'était pas son cousin." " By this day month they will probably be here; then shall I be happier than if His Majesty King George IV. were to give orders that I should be clothed in purple and sleep upon gold, and have a chain upon my neck, and sit next him because of my wisdom, and be called his cousin." When he had formed his Spanish and Portuguese collections, and his daughters had clothed in colored stuffs his pamphlets, which filled a room called "The Cottonian Library," and a book-room on the ground floor called "Paul" was furnished with volumes taken from an organ-room called "Peter," neither the offer of a baronetcy nor £2000 a year for a daily article in the "Times" could tempt him to leave Keswick.

In his "Colloquies":

"Why, Montesinos, with these books and the delight you take in their constant society, what have you to covet or desire?" asks Thomas More.

The reply is old-fashioned: "Nothing . . . except more books."

Montesinos should say now, "Better books." This "Holsome and Catholyke Doctryne" has a long note in the handwriting of Southey.

The Marquis de Morante collected "more books," and—like the learned Rufus, immortalized by Pliny the younger; Ebert, Director of the Dresden Library, canonized by Père Jacob; and the Hellenist Coray—fell from a ladder in his library-room and died. There are no shelves so elevated as to require a ladder in the private libraries of the decade.

There are the covers of calf, with arms of the Marquis de Morante and his legend, "J. Gomez de la Cortina et Amicorum," made by Petit for a "Hesiod," 1550, bought by the Marquis at the auction sale, in 1852, of the library of Gabriel Peignot. In the Peignot catalogue the book is No. 1259. There is the "Entomology," 1773, of Yeats, with marginal drawings in water-colors of every insect by Lady Aylesford.

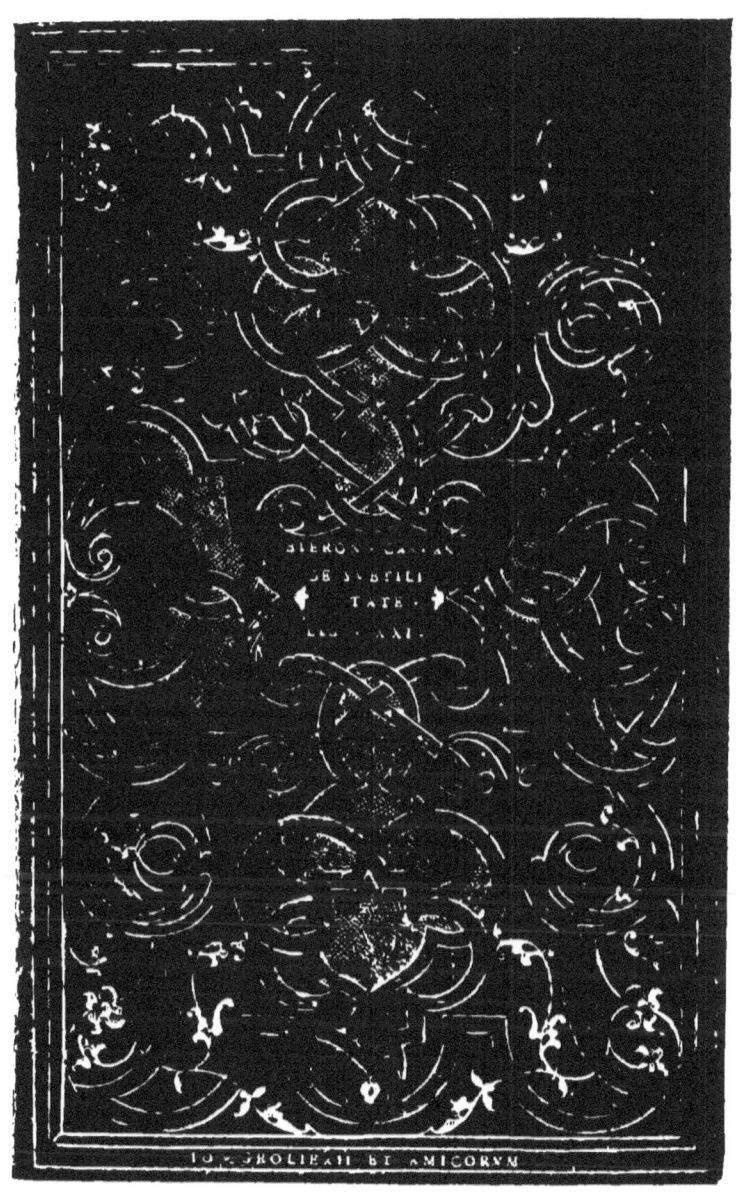

Photograph of front cover of Grolier's copy of Cardanus' De Subtilitate. See No. 230. (Size of original 12½ by 8 inches.)

It comes from the Aylesford auction sale. The covers are in green morocco studded with small stars in compartments, and lined with silk.

There are—but this chapter may be long continued. The collection is marvelous. All the styles of decoration of book-covers that are classified as Italian, Mosaic, Jansenist, Maïoli, Grolier, Eve, Le Gascon, Derome, and Roger Payne, are represented in it by perfect original examples. It contains all the art of bookbinding that the classicists knew. Excepting the covers of embroidered silk, which the classicists did not regard as examples of the art of bookbinding, what book-covers of the entire list are expressive of the books that they cover or accord with the definition of the decade? None. They are not dress, but a uniform or a livery. They are not the art of bookbinding, but the art of decorating book-covers of leather with marks of ownership or conventional designs.

BOOKS OF TO-DAY.

THERE are books of the decade that are famous. Philippe Burty invented some of them.

"L'Email des Peintres," 1866, of Claudius Popelin, poet and enameler, is dedicated to Burty,

> A dom Burty ce petit livre
> Rappellera mon souvenir ;
> J'estime que, s'il n'est pas ivre
> Il sera tenté de l'ouvrir.

It is bound in brown morocco, inlaid with an enamel, painted and gilded by Popelin, representing a genius treading on a serpent, and holding a ribbon inscribed with the title of the book. The enamel is signed with the monogram C. P. and dedicated "A mon ami Ph. Burty." The original drawings by Popelin for the enamel, and for all the vignettes, which Prunaire engraved, are inserted in the volume. The bookbinder is Petit.

"L'Art de l'Email," 1868, of Claudius Popelin, is bound in orange morocco, inlaid with a medallion in sgraffiti of gold by Popelin, signed, and with garnet morocco at the corners. The book contains an original drawing by Popelin of a reaper blowing a trumpet, with the legend: "A gens de village trompette de bois."

"De la Statue et de la Peinture," 1869, a translation by Claudius Popelin of the treatise of Alberti, is bound in red morocco, inlaid with an enamel by Popelin, signed, of the figure of the initial letter L of the prologue, representing a man on horseback. Burty has annotated the book. At the place where Popelin printed, "cet humble travail que j'ai fait aux heures dérobées sur mes petites affaires," Burty marked an asterisk referring to this note in pen and ink: "He wrote this book during the hours of night that he passed by the bedside of his wife, young and dying of a cancer in the breast." At the place where Popelin printed, "Naguères comme j'étais avec plusieurs hommes de bien tant peintres qu'écrivains, chez une noble dame," Burty wrote: "H. Taine, Paul de Saint Victor, E. et J. de Goncourt, Houssaye, Gautier, at the house of Mme. de Païva in the Champs-Elysées or in her lands of Pontchartrain."

"Cinq Octaves de Sonnets," 1875, of Claudius Popelin, is bound in green morocco, inlaid with an enamel of Popelin, signed, representing a reaper blowing a trumpet, and a ribbon inscribed: "A gens de village trompette de bois." The book contains an engraving by Flameng of Popelin's portrait in profile; an ex-dono, from Popelin to Burty: "Jam veteris amicitiæ pignus"; special impressions on China paper of the illustrations and autographs of the sonnets, printed in the book, of José Maria de Heredia, François Coppée, Théodore de Banville, and Anatole France. Also, this unpublished reply of Popelin to Heredia:

> Quand l'oxyde aura mis sur les plombs du ventail
> Sa morsure affamée, et que le froid des givres
> Sous sa flore enroulée aux méandres des guivres
> Aura fait éclater les feuilles du vitrail,
>
> Quand les blés jauniront les îles de corail,
> Quand les émaux figés sur le galbe des cuivres
> Auront été brisés par des lansquenets ivres,
> Quand la lime des temps aura fait son travail,

Les beaux sonnets inscrits sur le stèle d'ivoire,
De l'œuvre évanoui conserveront la gloire,
Afin de la narrer aux hommes qui vivront,

Et le bon ouvrier, sur le marbre des tombes
Gardera verdoyants, au fond des catacombes,
Les lauriers que l'oubli sècherait sur son front.

And this unpublished variant of the sonnet of Anatole France:

Claudius, tout nous trompe et tout n'est qu'apparence,
Mais la parole crée aux lèvres des devins
Un monde heureux, peuplé de fantômes divins,
Qui font aimer la vie et la vieille souffrance

La parole, O savant, combla ton espérance
Quand, d'un calme désir et loin des troubles vains,
Méditant le contour et l'essence, tu vins
A plier au sonnet le doux parler de France.

Tu le sais bien qu'il n'est qu'un œuvre et qu'un trésor,
Cher disciple d'Hermès à la baguette d'or;
Ceux-là seuls ont vécu qui surent voir les choses.

Retenons la beauté qui caresse nos yeux,
L'irrévocable Nuit, sur nos paupières closes
Est près d'appesantir son doigt silencieux.

This sonnet of Anatole France is written on a leaf, ruled with pale lines, torn from a memorandum-book; the sonnet of Théodore de Banville is written on an aristocratic, lily-white unruled leaf of Angoulême paper. Coppée and Popelin wrote on linen and drawing paper. José Maria de Heredia, in his large, superb, ancient calligraphy, on the fly-leaf, yellowed at the edge, of some antique book.

"Chefs d'Œuvre des Arts Industriels," of Philippe Burty, is bound in La Vallière morocco inlaid with an enamel by Popelin, signed, representing a vase, a chain, leaves, fruits, flowers, and marked "Arts Industriels."

"Les Ex-Libris Français," 1875, of Poulet-Malassis, is bound in green morocco inlaid with the plate of iron damascened, gilded, of Philippe Burty's ex-libris. Inserted in the book are the book-plates of Champfleury, Asselineau, Manet, Monselet, Fillon, Hozier, Queen Victoria, Sauvageot, Gambetta, Galichon, Paul de Saint Victor, and several autograph letters relative to the publication of the book.

In the "Châtiments," in one of the most splendid pages of the French language, the poet addressed the bees embroidered with threads of gold on the imperial mantle:

> Chastes buveuses de rosée,
> Qui, pareilles à l'épousée,
> Visitez le lys du coteau,
> O sœurs des corolles vermeilles,
> Filles de la lumière, abeilles,
> Envolez-vous de ce manteau!

When the Empress Eugénie quitted the Tuileries and the gates of the garden were opened before the Revolution, Philippe Burty marched into the palace and aided, with a pocket-knife, literal obedience to Hugo's figurative invocation. The "Châtiments," 1853, is bound in green morocco inlaid with one of the imperial bees liberated by Burty.

The book is one of twenty-two copies on China paper, and has this inscription on the fly-leaf: "Exilium vita est. A M. Ph. Burty, son ami Victor Hugo," in the poet's handwriting.

Another famous book of the decade is one invented by Poulet-Malassis. It is the immortal work of Baudelaire, the "Fleurs du Mal," wherein love and suffering exhale their intoxicating perfumes. It is illuminated with original drawings, etchings, and a letter of Bracquemond, and a note by Champfleury. There are an etched portrait of Baudelaire, five essays in pencil and aqua fortis of a frontispiece, thirty-three typographical ornaments, wood-engravings by Sotain, and Champfleury's comment:

By these frontispieces, these head- and tail-pieces, one may perhaps obtain a clearer idea of the 'Fleurs du Mal' than by reading them. Ordered and engraved under the direction of an editor, friend of the author, who had entered deeply into the workings of his mind, these vignettes were never published for various reasons. . . .

Bracquemond's letter, addressed to Champfleury, says:

I have just finished for the fifth time a skeleton-tree. But it is not yet the thing wanted. Malassis has one in view, and as long as I shall not have found it he will make me do the work again. He said you had the book which contained the skeleton of his dreams. I cannot recollect the name of the draughtsman. . . .

Bracquemond's five essays of a frontispiece were rejected, but his typographical ornaments, headings of chapters, initial ornate letters and tail-pieces were as Malassis wished them.

The headings have the initials of Baudelaire, C. B., and his devices; there are fleurons formed of a skull, snakes and wings of bats, flaming suns, expressed with the most charming delicacy of Bracquemond. "Le Livre Moderne," of March, 1891, contained reproductions of a heading, a letter N, and two of the frontispieces.

The "Salon," 1846, of Baudelaire—he signed his name in full, then, Baudelaire-Dufaÿs—is bound in La Vallière morocco, with the initials at each angle of a triangle, and the device, in the center, of Poulet-Malassis: "Pauci Boni Nitidi." Poulet-Malassis was one of the first to recognize a great poet in Baudelaire. In his lifetime they were only poets—Sainte-Beuve, Théophile Gautier, Théodore de Banville—and booklovers—Charles Asselineau, Poulet-Malassis—who appreciated him. The sentiment of the Greek sculptor about the shoemaker and his last never had greater provocation for its expression. The work of the artist was sincere, superb, animated by love of perfection, ardently disdainful of the commonplace; and the commonplace, and the frivolous triumphant in Jules Janin, were his critics. He had an incalculable treasure of book-lore in a mind profound, armed with locks and secrets as are minds refined. He was the son of a noble woman, everywhere admired, twice married and twice the wife of an ambassador. He entered life by the most dazzling of golden gates, wisely spent three fortunes in obtaining from it real and not hearsay impressions, and learned to envy nothing and to love the ideal. He was never in poverty, he had no bitterness of heart, his most intimate friend was Théodore de Banville, and Banville guarded jealously his invincible attachment for the beautiful. Yet legends have made Baudelaire depraved; the unfortunates who never understand anything having taken for his portrait the mirror, framed in leaves, flowers, and learned arabesques, wherein are reflected the faces of the passers-by.

About the woman who was Baudelaire's Laura, Paul Bourget has written: "The visage, shiny as ebony, of a friend with teeth of ivory, with kinky hair, inspired that litany of tenderness. . . ." It is a fair example of the legends about Baudelaire. Jeanne was a colored girl, but only a Creole might have discovered this by the telltale line marked on the nails of the octoroons. She was white—white as Gladys of Paul Bourget's "Pastels."

Mr. Avery has these books of Philippe Burty, these books of Poulet-Malassis, and many books of his invention. "Embroidery and Lace," 1888, of Ernest Lefébure, is bound in silk embroidery by Miss May Morris, daughter of the poet William Morris. "La Faïence," 1887, of Théodore Deck, is bound in brown morocco inlaid with faïence of Deck. On a fly-leaf Deck has written:

This book is a fruit that has taken forty years to ripen. Enjoy it with sentiment and reflection.

"Les Emaux Cloisonnés," 1868, of Philippe Burty, is bound in brown morocco inlaid with ancient Chinese cloisonné enamel. It is a dedication copy from Burty, and contains an original design by Régamey. "Marvels of Glass-making in All Ages," 1870, of A. Sauzy, is bound in dark-green morocco inlaid with glass panels designed in colors, enameled by Brocard. "Notes sur les Cuirs de Cordoue," 1878, of Davillier, is bound in imitation of ancient leather of Spain, by Quinet. "L'Email des Peintres," 1866, of Claudius Popelin, is bound in black morocco inlaid with an enamel by Thesmar, representing the genius of enamel with accessories, in the style of Limoges. It is a vellum copy.

"Jacques le Fataliste," 1884, of Diderot, is bound in purple morocco, in mosaic of gold and leather of various colors, forming scrolls, garlands, Cupids, graceful as the style of Diderot, three of whom, white as lilies, pink as leaves of mother-of-pearl, carry a ribbon on which the book-title is charmingly lettered. The bookbinder is Magnin of Lyons, rewarded with the gold medal at the Paris Exhibition of 1889. The book, printed for the Amis des Livres, contains two aquarelles of Maurice Leloir.

The "Contes Drolatiques," 1855, of Balzac, illustrated by Doré, contains a photograph of Doré, under which the artist has written:

On parle de ma facilité à dessiner, j'envierai cependant toujours celle du soleil.

As Mr. Avery was going out of the studio he heard the affectionate question of Doré's dear old mother shouted from the top of the stairs, " Gustave, est-ce que tu as fait des affaires ?"

"Manuel de l'Amateur de Reliures," 1887, of Léon Gruel, is bound by Léon Gruel in maroon morocco decorated in compartments of gilt lines. The "Art of Bookbinding," 1880, of Jos. W. Zaehnsdorf, is bound by Zaehnsdorf in brown morocco decorated with a Maïoli design, and inlaid at the center of the cover with red and green leather. "La Reliure Française," 1880, of Marius-Michel, is bound in brown morocco covered with a design of the Renaissance ungilt. "Modern Bookbinding Practically Considered," 1889, of William Matthews, is bound in citron morocco with examples of various styles of ornamentation in compartments: Grolier and

Eve on the front cover, Le Gascon and Roger Payne on the reverse cover, surrounded by a border of laurel. The book is one of three copies printed on vellum for the Grolier Club. These realizations of their own ideals by bookbinders on their own manuals are instructive and edifying. Comparisons are odious, but *tant pis!* If Marius-Michel had the grace of Matthews; if Matthews gilded as well as Marius-Michel, or only as well as Léon Gruel; if Zaehnsdorf had the *feu sacré* of either Marius-Michel, Matthews, or Gruel, there would be four perfect books of the decade, for these express perfectly their classicism, and the decade acclaims classicism perfectly expressed. I have turned the covers, decorated with gilt too pale and letters too ordinary, of the book of Matthews, and it was as if Faust, suddenly throwing off his dark mantle, appeared in dress of a cavalier. These covers are lined in apple-green morocco, inlaid with crimson, lemon, and orange, resplendent in a graceful and seductive design. This design is neither gilded nor lettered. "La Reliure Moderne," 1887, of Octave Uzanne, No. 1 of the Japan-paper copies, is bound by Ruban in citron morocco inlaid with designs emblematic of bookbinding: a book of the decade bound by an ardent artisan of the decade. "Histoire des Quatre Fils Aymon," 1883, is bound in brown morocco inlaid with leather incised and painted by Meunier, representing the four heroes on horseback with their lances and armor in silver. "Les Orientales," 1882, illustrated by Gérome and Constant, is bound by Joly in blue morocco, covered, by the use of thirty-six tools made expressly, with a mosaic of red, green, black, and white, forming the roses, arabesques, and festoons of the Orientals. The book was printed for the Amis des Livres. It is the only quarto book of the society's collection. It is ornamented

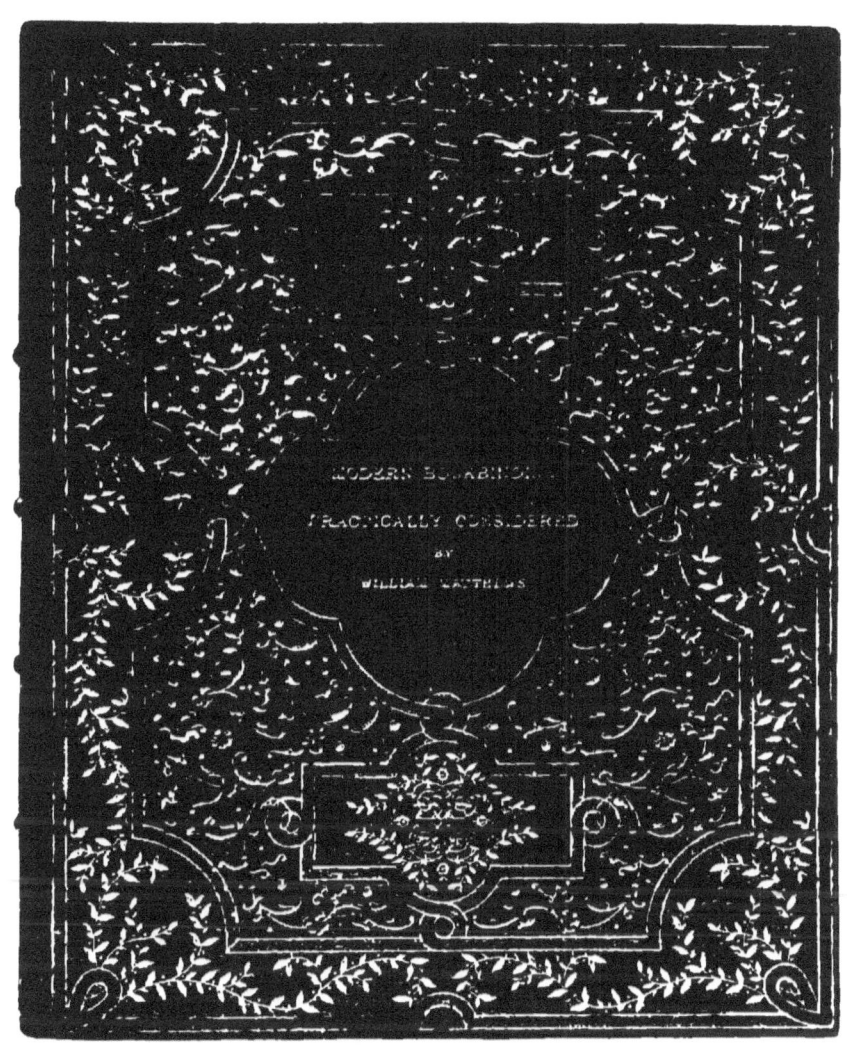

GROLIER CLUB PUBLICATION, 1889.
BINDING BY THE AUTHOR, WILLIAM MATTHEWS.

on a fly-leaf with the head of a calif, drawn by Benjamin Constant, and this autograph :

Ce livre fut mon premier rêve d'Orient, mon premier voyage au pays des Kalifes, et quand je le lus pour la première fois, alors que j'avais 15 ou 16 ans . . . je me sentis orientaliste pour la vie ! Benjamin Constant.

Underneath is this autograph:

J'écris avec grand plaisir mon nom à la première page de ce livre, un des plus remarquables du grand poète, œuvre faite de soleil, de jeunesse et d'azur, qui nous a initiés au monde oriental jusqu'alors couvert d'un voile, et nous en a montré toute la poésie. J. S. Gérome.

" At the Sign of the Lyre," 1885, has original illustrations in water-colors in the margins by A. Brennan. " Songs and Ballads," Book Fellows' Club, 1884, by Edmund Clarence Stedman, has this additional stanza to " The Old Picture-Dealer" :

> And yet — and yet, might time decree
> That Avery should my fame restore,
> That hovering shade would smile to see
> His Virgin shrined as ne'er before !
> Then, for one votary at my throne,
> The world should worship in his stead,
> And with its proffered gold atone
> For long neglect through centuries sped.

This additional stanza is in the handwriting and with the signature of Edmund Clarence Stedman.

The "Voyage Sentimental," illustrated by Leloir, has its illustrations washed in sepia by the artist, and this graceful autograph :

En souvenir des bonnes relations de Monsieur Avery avec mon frère et moi, je me fais un plaisir de faire pour lui de cet ouvrage un exemplaire unique, en rehaussant au lavis toutes les gravures dans le texte. Maurice Leloir. Paris, 1887.

"Les Chiens et les Chats," 1888, of G. de Cherville, illustrated by Eugène Lambert, contains original drawings of a cat in a cage, and one on a great folio, by the artist, original sketches, pictures, and etchings, not used, and this autograph:

Très heureux, Monsieur Avery, de vous dédier ce livre. L. Eug. Lambert.

"Nos Oiseaux," 1886, of André Theuriet, illustrated by Giacomelli, is bound in blue morocco by Ruban. The covers are decorated with a branch of lilacs, birds, and butterflies in mosaic of their most charming colors. The linings are of dark-blue morocco, inlaid with a garland of pinks and stems around a red panel. The guards are of blue silk embroidered. The book is on Japan paper, and contains an aquarelle, an exquisite composition of Giacomelli, wherein a medallion of S. P. Avery is surrounded by birds, leaves, flowers, and books.

The "Mémoires de Grammont," 1888, contains an aquarelle by Charnay, representing a woman standing before the gate of his garden, and this autograph :

A Monsieur Avery, hommage bien affectueux et souvenir de la dernière visit de son cher fils Henry à mon jardin de Marlotte, en août, 1889. A. Charnay.

Also an aquarelle by the illustrator of the book, with this inscription:

Souvenir affectueux de l'auteur des dessins à Monsieur Avery. C. Delort.

There is a little book of Ernest d'Hervilly, the wittiest of poets, author of this verse that Banville applauded:

> Les sergents de ville
> Qui s'en vont deux à deux, comme Dante et Virgile.

And of an allusion to persons whom everything astonishes,

> Ainsi qu'un éléphant à l'aspect d'une agrafe.

It is "Le Harem," 1874, for which Henry Somm had agreed to furnish illustrations. He began, and for reasons of a Bohemian, prodigious as d'Hervilly's wit, he never finished his work. The book contains the original illustrations which he made, and his excuses and explanations. It contains, also, original verses of d'Hervilly dedicated to Mr. George A. Lucas, friend of Mr. Avery, and a lover of art esteemed by all the artists of France.

There is "L'Epée et les Femmes," 1881, written by Edouard de Beaumont, illustrated by Meissonier, a large-paper copy, containing a drawing by Beaumont of one of his finest swords, with these words:

Juin, 1882. Cher Monsieur Avery. Avec tous mes bons souvenirs je vous adresse le portrait de *Martine*, une de mes quarante que vous ne connaissez pas.

There is Irving's "Knickerbocker's History of New-York," 1886, Grolier Club edition, bound by Zaehnsdorf in Dutch orange morocco, gilded at the edges over water-colors of landscapes of New Amsterdam by George H. Boughton. The volumes contain original drawings by Boughton, and poems in the handwriting of Robert Browning, Andrew Lang, William Black, and Austin Dobson. The following is by Dobson:

>Shade of Herrick, Muse of Locker,
>Help me sing of Knickerbocker!
>Boughton, had you bid me chant
>Hymns to Peter Stuyvesant!
>Had you bid me sing of Wouter,
>He, the onion-head, the doubter!
>But to rhyme of this one,— Mocker!
>Who shall rhyme to Knickerbocker?
>Nay, but where my hand must fail,
>There the more shall yours avail;
>You shall take your brush and paint
>All that ring of figures quaint—
>All those Rip Van Winkle jokers,
>All those solid-looking smokers,
>Pulling at their pipes of amber,
>In the dark-beamed Council Chamber.
>
>Only art like yours can touch
>Shapes so dignified . . . and Dutch;
>Only art like yours can show
>How the pine logs gleam and glow,
>Till the fire-light laughs and passes
>'Twixt the tankards and the glasses,
>Touching with responsive graces
>All those grave Batavian faces —
>Making bland and beatific
>All that session soporific.

VOLUME THE First

SPECIALLY DRAWN BY GEO. H. BOUGHTON FOR S. P. AVERY'S
"KNICKERBOCKER'S HISTORY OF NEW-YORK."

Then I come and write beneath,
Boughton, he deserves the wreath;
He can give the form and hue —
This the Muse can never do!

The following is by William Black:

Dear friend,
Of all good things you 're most deserving,
But this appeal is quite un-Irving;
The only Knickerbockers *I* know
Are those made up and sold by Kino;
And where 's the link 'twixt New-York history
And grouse and salmon; that 's the mystery!
I give it up: I have no text!
I cannot preach! call on the next!

The following is by Andrew Lang:

ALMA QUIES.

How I wish upon the whole
I 'd been fated
To have lived when not a soul
"Agitated"!
That my birth had but occurred
In a Nation
Where they did not know the word
"Demonstration"!

Andrew Lang might be charmed with New-York. Like it, the Avery books are full of the smiles of fairies. In letters that have the tenuity of their lips, smaller than the thinnest sparks of a ruby cut by a lapidary, they are the miniature classics of Pickering, fables of La Fontaine, tales of Florian, maxims of La Rochefoucauld, a setting of humorous poetry in brilliant types by Theodore L. De Vinne, made expressly for Viviane, Morgana, the great Mélusine, and Queen Titania. The illustrious fairies, in gowns of diamond thread and sapphire weaved, read them. In the murmur of springs, in the shiver of leaves, it is reminiscences of "Horatii Opera," 1824, in blue morocco inlaid with lyre and laurel, that one hears. In the tempest, stanzas that tear the skies terrified are from "Poésies" of Victor Hugo, a relic of the National Exhibition of Brussels, 1880, thus indorsed, in Hugo's handsomest calligraphy:

Je remercie les auteurs de ce chef-d'œuvre typographique, et je les prie de me croire leur ami. Victor Hugo. 29 Juillet, 1880.

There are, in fairy typography, "Verbum Sempiternum," 1693, of John Taylor, the Water-Poet; "Maximes," 1827, of La Rochefoucauld, the font for which was made by Henri Didot at the age of sixty-six years; "El Libro de Misa de los Niños"; the "Estelle" of Florian; "Le Rime di Petrarca," 1879; almanacs, calendars, and diaries of the eighteenth century, one of which, in Dutch, contains tales of Boccaccio, and is bound in two sheets of mother-of-pearl; "Les Bucoliques de Cythère"; "De Imitatione Christi," 1858; "Horace," 1828; "Vert-Vert" and other poems, 1855, bound by Canapé-Belz, with the parrot inlaid in its natural colors; the "Finger New Testament"; the "Fairy Annual" of 1838; the "Quads," that Tuer called, by a prodigious abuse of authority, "Midget Folio"; "Amour et Gloire," 1827; Schloss's "English Bijou Almanac," 1841, the measurement of which is five eighths of an inch in width by one half inch in length. In fairy books it is not the measurement of the pages that counts, for De Vinne observes justly: "The smallest book I have ever seen is about one half inch in width and one inch in length, but its type was of the size nonpareil, and the words were of one syllable." I give the measurement of Schloss's book because it is the smallest of the fairy books. In the preface to the well-named "Brilliants," 1888, of De Vinne, one learns that 2304 types of "n," or 3456 types of "l" of the book are required to make the weight of one pound. Before this lesson of the decade, book-collectors made no discrimination, in classifying fairy books, in favor of books printed. With them the "Paul et Virginie," a photographic reduction published by Flammarion, might have passed for a fairy book, as passed a book engraved. The book-collectors were not book-lovers.

There are the books written, engraved, and published by W. J. Linton. They are "Bob-Thin; or, The Poorhouse Fugitive," 1845, which has on a fly-leaf, in the handwriting of Joseph Mazzini, this inscription:

A George Sand; en témoignage d'admiration pour son génie et de sympathie pour ses croyances, l'auteur par l'entremise de votre ami dévoué, Joseph Mazzini."

And this explanation:

Printed by me at 85 Hatton Gardens, London. Given by me to my friend Mazzini for presentation to Madame Sand. W. J. Linton.

"The Plaint of Freedom," 1852; "Claribel and Other Poems," 1865; "Voices of the Dead"; "Famine: A Masque"; "Pot-Pourri"; "Ireland for the Irish," 1867; "England to America: A New-Year's Greeting," 1876; "The Princes' Noses: A

Modern Idyl," A. Tennyson; "Cetewayo and Dean Stanley";
"James Watson: A Memoir," 1879; " Rare Poems of the Sixteenth and Seventeenth Centuries: A Supplement to the Anthologies," 1882; "Golden Apples of Hesperus," 1882, with autograph of R. H. Stoddard, to whom the book is dedicated, and autograph and several original drawings, descriptive of the Appledore press, of W. J. Linton; "The American Odyssey," 1876; "Harry Marten's Dungeon Thoughts"; "The House that Tweed Built"; "Editorial Right: W. J. Linton vs. 'The Atlantic Monthly,'" 1879; "Slanderers," 1879; "Wild Flowers for Children, by Mr. Honeysuckle"; "In Dispraise of Woman," a verse of Catullus, with thirty-two variations by Linton, 1886, in light-brown morocco with a Grecian border inclosing the verse of Catullus in gilt letters, by Maillard; "Love-Lore," 1887; "Windfalls," 1886; Translations," 1881; "Poems and Translations," 1889, with this original poem, in the handwriting of Linton, addressed to Avery:

> And so, my friend! even in Love's courts you ask
> A place for Friendship. Are you serious then?
> And think your poet can resume his pen
> And use its gold nib on a lower task?
>
> For Love is above Friendship. Is it so?
> Methinks there is a scripture with the words,
> " Dearer than love of women," which affords
> Excuse for the assurance that you show.
>
> The warrant so accepted, let there be
> A corner and a welcome for the guest!
> So, wishing you whatever more is best,
> I waft you this admission o'er the sea.

There is one of the three copies, written, printed, and engraved at Appledore, by Linton, in 1884, of "The Masters of Wood-Engraving." It is the original edition, with original illustrations, of his crowning work.

At Appledore, under the shadow of East Rock, near New Haven, for a quarter of a century, William James Linton, now in his eightieth year, "and not ashamed," as he writes in an ex-dono, has lived in his elevated ideal. Engraver, poet, political writer; in his youth a zealous Chartist; the friend of Mazzini; the ardent, enthusiastic editor of "The English Republic"; the poet eulogized by Landor; the engraver upon whom has fallen the mantle of Bewick,— Linton has not had a thought, he has not done an act, that Art would wish effaced. It is a glory of our country that it has Linton; it is in the Avery library only that one may find the books of Linton.

There is an album filled with notes, long letters, circulars, memoranda, received and written by Méryon. There is a little pocket-album, filled with drawings, paintings, autographs, lyrism, of the greatest contemporary artists. On the first page Detaille has drawn an aquarelle representing himself on horseback, in his uniform of a Garde Mobile during the war with Germany. At every page is an interesting, intimate note like this from artists to Mr. Avery, from celebrated men to their patron and friend.

There are twelve thousand etchings, engravings, lithographs, photographs of paintings, of the nineteenth century; many art-books and illustrated catalogues; hundreds of autograph letters and original sketches by artists living and dead; two hundred historic and artistic medals in gold, silver, and bronze; etchings, classified alphabetically in portfolios, of two hundred and eighty-two artists. There are nine hundred and seventy etchings by Bracquemond, six hundred and forty by Flameng, six hundred and twenty-five by Geurard, five hundred and ninety-seven by Jacque, four hundred and twelve by Martial, four hundred and eight by Jacquemart, two hundred and eighty-six by Lalanne, two hundred and sixty-five by Rajon, two hundred and fifty-three by Buhot, two hundred and thirty-nine by Courtry, two hundred and twenty-six by Goeneutte, two hundred and twenty by Seymour Haden, two hundred and eight by Whistler, one hundred and ninety-five by Zilcken, one hundred and seventy-six by Daubigny, one hundred and sixty-two by Unger, one hundred and twenty-three by Méryon, one hundred and ten by Gravesende, one hundred and one by Chauvel; collections in bound volumes, as the publications of the "English Etching Club" — a tower of masterpieces, proofs in various states, signed, retouched, marked in the margins by the artists with their portraits and affectionate dedications. I have enumerated them as one attempts to enumerate the stars and constellations in a rage of realism.

THE ELZEVIRS.

I<small>T</small> is an easy ascent from indifference to an artistic piety intolerant and jealous for the Elzevir books. The indifference comes of their popularity as books traditionally valuable, the apparent familiarity with them in persons not book-lovers, the frequency of their occurrence in lists of books classically scarce. The art of the decade inspires a horror of the conventional, and conventional was praise of them until they were illuminated by the triumphant art of the decade. Conventional, mechanical, as if made to order, the praise of Brunet and Bérard; financially interested the praise of Motteley; unintelligent the praise of Brunet, Bérard, Motteley, Pieters, because it made valuable as many false as authentic books of the Elzevirs. I recollect perfectly that I wrote, after a siege of pseudo-Elzevirians: "A great temptation is to collect the Elzevir books, upon which has been wasted a good deal of sentimentality. They are of a dainty size; the paper, the distinct black type, the occasional frontispiece, are seductive in the extreme, but the beauty is at the surface. At its best, the text is full of errors." This happened many years ago, and now, instructed by Alphonse Willems and initiated into mysteries that I had not even suspected, I amend my sentence, as a legislator might say, by inserting the word "false" before the word "Elzevirs." Thus I shall not be troubled with a ghost of my Record.

The founder of the family was Louis Elzevir. He was born at Louvain, about 1540. He was a bookbinder at Antwerp, and occasionally worked at his trade for Plantin, when the Duke of Alba came to cure heresy by force of arms. A Protestant, he went into exile in Holland. In 1581 he was a bookbinder of Leyden; two years later, a bookseller indebted to Plantin of Antwerp; in 1617, when he died, a great merchant, admired in all the principal cities of Europe. In 1617 his grandson Isaac had been for a year the owner of a printing-press; his sons Louis and Gilles at The Hague, his son Josse at Utrecht, his sons Bonaventure and Matthew at Leyden, had aided him valiantly and were established in reputation as booksellers.

Isaac was the son of Matthew. In 1621 his elder brother Abraham, the greatest typographer of the family, and his uncle Bonaventure, were associated with him in the production of books. He retired in 1625. The printing-house of Leyden recruited in 1652 Daniel, son of Elizabeth, who stayed three years and then became an associate of his cousin Louis, son of Gilles, owner since 1638 of a book-shop and printing-house at Amsterdam. The son of Abraham, John, continued the work of the printing-house at Leyden until 1661; the Amsterdam house lasted until 1680. The Leyden house was managed by the wife of John until 1681, when his son Abraham assumed charge of it and let it fall into ruins. There is not in the chronicles of kingdoms a more edifying record.

Louis Elzevir is a perfect representative of the men who founded a transoceanic Novum Belgium. He was sincere, laborious, enterprising although not adventurous, and practical to the full extent of the immense horizons that the word practical may evoke. He gave nothing to the gods of Hellas, and expected nothing from them; he had faith in his work, and if the University had not aided him, after fourteen years of tribulations at Leyden, he would not have become, as he then became, in 1594 only, a citizen, a " poorter" of Leyden. Perhaps the description printed at Amsterdam, in 1655, of the native inhabitants of New Netherland, written by Van der Donck, owner of an estate on the Hudson near Yonkers, would have been printed at the Elzevir Press in New Amsterdam! The Elzevir Press was an irresistible evolution, and not in the least dependent on its surroundings. The printers of Holland addressed Holland; the Elzevirs communicated with the world. The Elzevir Press would have been created in New Amsterdam, where there were only tradespeople, as well as at Leyden, where there were men of learning and a university.

Christopher Van Dyck invented and engraved the Elzevir types. He was utterly unknown before the art of the decade, represented by Alphonse Willems, unearthed at the Plantin-Moretus Museum of Antwerp his titles to fame, gravely accorded by Didot in his stead to Garamond and to Sanlecque. These titles are in the form of a letter from the widow of Daniel Elzevir to the widow of Moretus, dated January 3, 1681, accompanied by a catalogue of the Elzevir types with the name of their inventor, the letter praising the inventor.

The occasion for it was the sale by auction, March 5, 1681, of all the tools and types of the Elzevirs. Less than a hundred years later, the work of Van Dyck was extinct, destroyed or refounded into other types, but the books that had been printed with them are indestructible. Ménage appreciated this in 1663, when Daniel Elzevir published an edition of his poems, " Ægidii Menagii Poemata," for he added to the collection a poem in Latin to the publisher:

Gods and Goddesses, what do I see! My verses reproduced in Elzevirian type! O types elegant and exquisite! O graceful and charming volume! The tiny letters rival pitch in blackness, the paper is equally white as snow. . . . Thus decked the volume attracts and holds, whether he wishes or not, the reader! The types lend to my verses charms that they had not. They are as a bride to whom a skilful hairdresser gives charms that Fate had denied to her. But you, Elzevir, my sweet glory, you the father of these most elegant types, what may I offer to you in return for such a gift? May the book-lovers ever prefer your works! May buyers fill your shop! May the name of Elzevir, transmitted from age to age by the voice of poets, fill earth and heaven! May you surpass Turnebus and Vascosan, vanquish Stephanus and Manutius!

I like Ménage because he was pedantic; because there are forty pieces dedicated to Mme. de La Fayette, and only five dedicated to Mme. de Sévigné, in his "Poemata"; because Tallemant des Réaux was jealous of him; and because he praised Elzevir. I like to think of Heinsius and his letter to Thévenot about the " Virgil " of 1676:

My edition is depreciated in the view of many persons who do not admit the propriety of inclosing the prince of poets in a frame so small. I have had to submit against my will to the exigencies of the typographer. You will recognize in this, with your habitual equity, the inveterate malady of our booksellers, who are after nothing but money, and have no regard for the dignity of letters.

Is it not amusing? Who would know Heinsius if it were not for the Elzevir " Virgil" that he disdains so superbly? Assuredly, only the gravest men of erudition. But the "Virgil" of 1676 is a book of to-day. The text of it is a model ; the only serious errors noted by J. Chenu are *tigri* for *Tigri*, p. 282, v. 166 ; *omibus* for *omnibus*, p. 296, v. 691 ; *fotunam* for *fortunam*, p. 352, v. 920. The only errors noted by Willems are *e-equidem* in the 9th line of the preliminary notice in the first impression; a period after *Fudit equum* in Georg. lib. i, v. 13; *tela* for *tecta* in Æn. iv, v. 260. The work has an interesting history. It was in the press while France and the United Provinces were at war. Heinsius dedicated it to Louis XIV., but the impropriety of making the dedication public delayed for three years, until peace was achieved, the appearance of forty-eight copies printed on large paper. In September, 1676, appeared the duodecimo "Virgil," measuring about 148 millimeters, containing 24 preliminary leaves, including the engraved title ; 387 pages; 29 pages, not numbered, for table of contents ; a blank leaf and a map of Æneas's navigation. In 1679, but with date of 1676 unaltered, appeared copies of the duodecimo " Virgil," measuring about 184 millimeters, and copies of the ordinary height, which were copies unsold since 1676, containing two additional leaves, inserted after the title-page and before the preliminary notice. These additional leaves contained the epistle to Louis XIV. Heinsius presented one of the large-paper copies to the King, and another to the Dauphin, bound in levant morocco with an elaborate tooling of dotted lines with lace border, four crowns, and twelve fleurs-de-lis, all gilt, by Magnus, a bookbinder of Amsterdam.

In the library of Mr. George Beach de Forest, in mere contemplation of the Elzevir books, the hours fly wildly as if a furious god chased them with whips through the vast azure. There is the "Cæsar" of 1635, 12mo, one copy in old morocco with monogram of Canon Digby, and one copy in red morocco with gilt lines, in the style affected by Duseuil. The paper, the type, the ornaments, the engraved title, the maps, the accurate text, enchant. Willems says that it is "the greatest book of the Elzevirs," and the best alcade is the King. But there is the "Imitatione Christi," not dated, 12mo, bound by Cuzin. It bears the imprint:

Lugduni, apud Joh: et Dan: Elsevirios.

"Batavorum" never appeared on the title-page of Elzevir books printed for sale in Catholic countries; John and Daniel were in partnership from the end of 1652 to May, 1655, and they printed Corneille's version of the "Imitation" in 1653, so that the "Imitatione" may be ascribed to the year 1653. It is a jewel. The Elzevirs of Amsterdam tried in vain to reproduce it in their dated edition of 1658. Like an arrow, a book may or may not strike the same point twice, however surely aimed. Reprinted twice in 1635, the original "Cæsar" is perfect, the first reprint is admirable, and the second reprint is passable. The original is easily distinguished by comparison with the reprints; or by the head-piece to the dedication and to page 1, which is a buffalo-head, and by errors in the numbering of pages 149, 335, and 475. They are numbered 153, 345, and 375. The head-piece to the dedication of the first reprint is a siren, and page 238 is numbered by error 248. The second reprint has 4 instead of 12 preliminary leaves, 526 pages of 37 lines instead of 561 pages of 35 lines, and 17 instead of 70 unnumbered leaves of index.

There is the "Seneca" of 1640, in red morocco lined with red morocco, marked on the covers at the center and corners, and on the backs, in gilt, with the emblem used by the chivalric Order of the Golden Fleece. Longepierre, a marquis of the last century, and a pale playwright, adopted that emblem after he had obtained a quasi-triumph with his "Médée." The play is not good. The emblem is prettily decorative, but it is not emblematic of Longepierre, marquis; nor of Longepierre, playwright; nor of the philosophy of Seneca. Nevertheless, Longepierre was a great book-collector, and the handicraft of the book-covers made for him is excellent.

There is the "Cicero" of 1642, in olive morocco lined with red morocco, once the property of La Roche-La Carelle. There are the "Commines" of 1648, in red morocco, with fleurs-de-lis at the corners by Trautz-Bauzonnet, formerly the property of Paillet; the "Pharsale de Lucain," 1658, in red morocco, by Trautz-Bauzonnet, formerly owned by L. de Montgermont; the "Gallerie des Femmes Fortes," 1660, in covers by Derome, formerly in the Marquis collection. There are the "Sagesse" of Charron, the edition not dated, less beautiful but scarcer than the edition of 1656 which it copied, changing only the dedication; the "Boccaccio," 1665, in blue morocco, wrongly attributed by Brunet to the press of Blaeu; the "Horace" of 1629, in brown morocco; the "Horace" of 1676, 12mo, in red morocco, formerly in the Hamilton Palace collection; the "Livy" of 1678, in red morocco, by Trautz-Bauzonnet, all the history of Titus-Livius in one volume — merciful Elzevirs!

There is the turbulent "Pastissier François," 1655, in citron morocco lined with blue morocco, with compartments of straight and curved lines on the covers, with dotted lines on the lining, gilt, by Trautz-Bauzonnet, and the very copy which caused the turbulence, the copy that Ernest Quentin-Bauchart sold for 4600 francs, as if francs were notes based, as financiers of the Wild West say, on unborn herds of buffaloes in undiscovered prairies.

There is the "Aimable Mère de Jésus," incomparably scarcer, 1671, in green morocco, inlaid with a silver lily and lined in white vellum, with angels and stars gilt, by Ruban. The special cause for the scarcity of the book may be found in "L'Edit du Roy pour le Règlement des Imprimeurs et Libraires de Paris," published by Thierry in 1687. The fifth article of the edict enjoined booksellers and printers from using fictitious names of booksellers; an example of its enforcement is given in "the book having for title 'L'Aimable Mère de Jésus,' and at the foot 'printed at Amiens by the Widow Hubault, with privilege,' and the said book was printed at Amsterdam by Daniel Elzevir." The entire consignment received at Amiens was confiscated. The imprint is not exactly reproduced in "L'Edit." It is: "A Amiens, pour la Veuve du [sic] Robert Hubant, ruë de Beaupuis, 1671. Avec Privilège du Roy." This was changed, in some copies that had not been sent to Amiens, into: "Seconde édition. A Cologne, et se vend à Paris chez Thomas Joly, 1677." This copy measures 137 millimeters, and is the tallest copy known.

"L'AIMABLE MÈRE DE JÉSUS," ELZEVIR, 1671.
BINDING INLAID WITH LILY OF SILVER, BY RUBAN.

There is the "Molière" of 1675, in red morocco with dotted lines gilt by Capé. This edition, formed of 26 plays published separately by Elzevir, has in its fifth volume a comedy of Brécourt, "L'Ombre de Molière," and "Les Intermèdes du Malade Imaginaire." "La Cocue Imaginaire," by Donneau de Visé, printed by Elzevir in 1662, is inserted. The pages measure 133 millimeters, and there are many witnesses — that is, uncut leaves: the French say *témoins* — to prove that the margins were not heedlessly reduced by the bookbinder.

Height of copies has been, for a longer time than book-collectors may suppose, and is fatally, an important consideration in Elzevir books. The inventory of La Gallissonnière, made in 1725 or thereabout, contained a "Cicero" of 1642, which brought, for the reason that it was uncut, the sum, fabulous for the time, of 200 francs. The "Regnier" of 1652, in the library of Mr. de Forest, in covers in mosaic, after a design of Padeloup by Trautz-Bauzonnet, is uncut.

Here it becomes necessary to open a very large parenthesis. A book bound, by an artist of the decade, in full morocco, may or may not be uncut, but it must be all gilt. A book bound in full morocco is finally bound; but the art of bookbinding is an art of the decade. The Elzevir editions were published with leaves fitted to covers in amazing uniformity. Then collectors caused them to be uncovered and recovered successively by various workmen, according to varying tastes. In the time before Trautz and Lortic every recovering entailed a reducing of margins. Trautz was not an artist of the decade, but he was a great artist in book-covers, and book-lovers regard as pure vandalism the discarding of Trautz covers. He might have cut the leaves of the "Regnier" of

1652, since he was making for it a marvel of the century — that is, covers in mosaic signed Trautz-Bauzonnet. It was one of twenty-two mosaics, twenty-two masterpieces, that he invented. He knew perfectly the value of his work; he was not less proud of it than José Maria de Heredia is of his sonnets. His traditions, his self-respect, his love of harmony, the assurance that he and collectors of Elzevirs had of the inviolability of his work for all time — everything induced his cutting of the leaves of the uncut "Regnier" of 1652. He preferred to give to the world a book twice marvelous: AN ELZEVIR GILT ON UNCUT EDGES IN MOSAIC COVERS OF TRAUTZ-BAUZONNET. Here closes the parenthesis.

The covers of the "Regnier" of 1652 are reproduced in gold and colors in the frontispiece to "Four Private Libraries of New-York." Their lining is of red morocco with lace border. I have reserved for the end of this chapter, "Description de la Ville d'Amsterdam en Vers Burlesques," because its dedicatory epistle will please the burgomasters of New Amsterdam:

A très vilains, très sales, très lourds, très malpropres et très ignorants Messieurs les boueurs et cureurs des canaux d'Amsterdam.

Until 1639, Bonaventure and Abraham Elzevir made use of a paper smaller than the paper used for the "Seneca" of 1640. The art of the decade gives 130 millimeters as the height of the tallest "Cæsar" of 1635 extant, and regards as extremely scarce copies of Elzevir books antedating the "Seneca," measuring more than 130 millimeters. The art of the decade decrees that Elzevir books of 1640 and after shall have from 133 to 138 millimeters in height, unless they happen to be volumes of Amsterdam like the "Baudii Epistolæ" of 1654 or the "Malebranche" or "St.-Disdier" of 1680, for these may measure 145 millimeters. Of course all this applies to duodecimo volumes. The others are not as firm in the affection of book-lovers.

Graceful, severe, correct, of a great epoch, the Elzevir books, as the art of the decade defines them in the manual of Willems, as they are chosen at present — not only with an Elzevirmeter, a purse of Fortunatus, and a copy of Willems, but with individual, special taste — have greater claims than ever before to enthusiastic appreciation. They are naïve, those who quote as if they were of surprising magnitude the thousands and thousands of francs brought by "L'Illustre Théâtre de M. Corneille," and the "Maximes" of La Rochefoucauld, books of the Elzevirs, at the sale of the Paillet library.

THE VIGNETTISTS.

Of the eighteenth century it is not the poetry that is precious. Voluptuous, its shepherds had in their veins rose-water; the gods that it made of the forces and energies of Nature were of soft paste. Its paganism was vague. It recited eclogues of love, madrigals, vows, romances; it served, as Musset said, milk and sugar in tender-green tights. In poems, Eglé had an inch of rouge on her cheeks, and Tircis wore garnet-colored bows at his knees.

In paintings, the personages divinely sad of Watteau wandering in the ideal, the Dianas of Boucher with chalky thighs whipped with red, the peasants and gallants of Lancret and Pater in dress of satin, proclaimed without effusion the religion of Life in the enchantment of dreams. They were marvelously drawn; they were prodigiously graceful.

At the Renaissance, when men returned to antiquity, after centuries of torture and painful relinquishment, it was Jules the Roman, it was the plastic arts that celebrated Aphrodite, the universal desire of gods and beasts, Danaë and the rain of gold, Leda palpitating under the kiss of the swan, the creative force that links in one chain all beings and things. In the eighteenth century in France, in an age of triumph and luxury, when men learned in all the arts, ennobled by battles, crowned with flowers, admired in women beautiful as goddesses matter spiritualized, it was again the arts of design and the plastic arts that expressed them.

Two book-lovers of the decade, Edmond and Jules de Goncourt, wrote of the art of the eighteenth century, and, in-

stantly, the "Départ pour Cythère," that the Académie des Beaux Arts had relegated into a corner of the studio of David's pupils, was placed into the Salon Carré of the Louvre. About the quarto edition of Voltaire's works, published in 1768, with prints by Gravelot, Grimm wrote:

It should have been a beautiful octavo edition; . . . it should have been without pictures, for these will soon destroy in France the taste for drawing and typography.

Voltaire wrote to Fyot de la Marche:

I have never liked prints in books: what does a woodcut matter to me when I am reading the second book of Virgil, and what graver may add anything to the description of the city of Troy?

Alas! the book-lovers of the decade would not have a work of Voltaire if it were not for the vignettists who have made some books of Voltaire valuable. Edmond and Jules de Goncourt picked them out of the fifteen-cent boxes of the parapets on the quays of Paris, as archæologists picked out of neglected graveyards figurines of Tanagra.

In turning the leaves of the books of the vignettists, in the library of Mr. de Forest, I have seen perfectly the garden of Watteau, and the boat where the martyrs of love embark for the sad and mad Cythera. There were Silvia and her valet Dorante, she divining that he was a marquis in disguise; Satan in pigeon-throat colored cloak; Columbine flirting with a black Scaramouch and a pink Mezzetin; and Eglé and Aminte. I have seen alleys of trees and flowers lengthened and enlarged into landscapes where shone silver lakes, where grew bowers of Le Nôtre bordered with white statues; a Pompadour with long train of dazzling brocade, worn expressly to be copied by Latour in a pastel ; comedians seated in the grass before a green curtain formed of antique trees ; women, in gowns of satin, singing while Gilles played the flute of Pan. A penetrating charm envelops with the immense sadness of joy the scenes and the personages.

The eighteenth century had not a pleiad of poets, but it had a pleiad of artists. They were the vignettists Eisen, Moreau, Gravelot, Boucher, Cochin, Marillier, and Choffart. In other constellations were other vignettists, and all were relatives of Watteau and Marivaux. There were some who were faithful copyists of costumes, and there were some who were not; there were those who reflected and those who illuminated; but they were all kindred of the painter of Comedy and of the author of "Marianne," and they amalgamated in ideal figures the theater and life. I know the profound science by which their work is classified in favor of students of human documents, in favor of psychologists, in favor of philosophers and moralists; but Perdican of Musset, who lived in their parks, where murmur leaves and sonorous fountains, expressed about flowers the impression that I have of vignettes in books of the eighteenth century. They are fragrant and beautiful, *voilà tout!* They are the lily and the rose, they are vignettes of the eighteenth century.

They are—on Holland paper—the illustrations made by Eisen for a translation of "Anacréon, Sapho, Bion et Moschus," 1773, augmented in this volume with opuscules of Musæus and Theocritus, 1774, also Gallicized by Moutonnet Clairfons, and the entire series of head- and tail-pieces of Eisen in artist proofs taken without text, impressions acute and brilliant as proofs of medals ; the illustrations made by Gravelot, Boucher, Cochin, and Eisen, for "Le Décaméron," 1757–

1761, in five volumes uncut, in covers by Trautz-Bauzonnet, proofs indorsed with a signature printed, augmented with the entire series of secret illustrations of Gravelot, etchings, and two states of the plate made for the first tale of the eighth day in the Italian edition printed in Paris in 1757. They are the illustrations made by Monnet and Moitte for the "Aventures de Télémaque," 1785, augmented with proofs of illustrations made by Marillier, Cochin, Moreau, and Boucher; those made by Gravelot for the "Tom Jones" of 1750, inserted in the French edition, translation of La Bédoyère, 1833; those made by Smirke, Marillier, and others for fairy tales, inserted in "Les Mille et Une Nuits," 1822-1825; and those made by Marillier for "Tangu et Félime," 1780. They are, on China paper, proofs of the illustrations made by Smirke, Marillier, and Desenne for "Gil Blas," inserted in the edition annotated by François de Neufchâteau aided by Hugo, a large-paper copy, 1820, in covers by the incomparable Lortic.

The frontispieces made by Cochin and Moreau, and the frontispiece, head- and tail-pieces, and illustrations in the text made by Eisen, for "Tarsis et Zélie," 1774. In three states, on vellum, the portrait of Montesquieu by Saint-Aubin, and the illustrations by Regnault and Le Barbier for "Le Temple de Gnide," 1795, in covers by Bozérian. Plates engraved by Le Mire, impressions with remarques before the rose, before the flag, and before the cloud of the illustrations made by Eisen for "Le Temple de Gnide," 1772, in covers of orange morocco, ornamented with roses and loving, cooing doves, by Trautz-Bauzonnet.

They are the illustrations made by Le Barbier for the "Chansons Nouvelles," 1785, augmented with the portrait of Piis engraved by Gaucher. The illustrations made by Pasquier and Le Bas for the "Manon Lescaut," 1753, on Holland paper; and, in proofs and etchings, those made by Lefèvre for the "Manon Lescaut," 1797. The illustrations made by Moreau and Freudeberg for "Tableaux de la Bonne Campagnie," 1787, uncut, in covers by Cuzin, augmented with the plate of the Boudoir made for a later edition, the illustrations made and published by Moreau under the title of "Seconde Suite d'Estampes pour Servir a l'Histoire des Modes et du Costume," and illustrations made by Freudeberg for an almanac of the time, in the state of proofs on special paper. The illustrations made by Lefèvre, proofs and etchings, for "Voyages de Gulliver," 1797, large paper, in covers ornamented at the back with a sailing vessel, by Bozérian, in a primitive, initial, touching ambition for symbolism. The illustrations made by Eisen for "Le Tableau de la Volupté," 1771, and for "La Pipe Cassée," in the state of artist proofs taken without text—a state unique. The illustrations made by Lefèvre for "Primerose," 1797, two copies, in one of which, in covers by Thibaron-Joly, are proofs and etchings.

The illustrations, unsigned, made probably by Eisen for twenty tales in verse, unknown to bibliographers, united under the title of "Vingt Contes en Vers," 1760; those made by Vigée and Queverdo for "Romans et Contes" of Voisenon, 1798, in the state of proofs on vellum paper; and, in proofs, the portraits by Saint-Aubin and pictures by Moreau for the Works of Voltaire. The proofs of the illustrations by Gérard and Prudhon for "Les Amours Pastorales de Daphnis et Chloé," 1800, on large vellum paper; augmented with proofs of the illustrations made by the Duke of Orleans and engraved by Audran for the edition called Regent; proofs and etchings of illustrations made by Le Barbier for an unpublished, unfinished edition; proofs on China paper and etchings of a series of illustrations by Prudhon, Gérard, and Hersent; proof and etching of an illustration of the bath of Daphnis, made by Prudhon for the duodecimo edition of Renouard; four lithographs of Prudhon's "Saisons," and many other illustrations, among which may be noted, in proof and in etching, the one of Pan made by Gravelot for the "Métamorphoses d'Ovide," 1767-1771. The frontispiece by Coypel, illustrations by the Duke of Orleans, engraving by Count Caylus called "Petits Pieds," illustration in the text by Scotin, and ornamented letters, made for the edition called Regent of "Les Amours Pastorales de Daphnis et Chloé," 1718. The "Petits Pieds" plate appeared in 1728; the edition of 1718 was reprinted in 1745. with date of the engraved frontispiece, 1718, unchanged; in the reprint the capital letters are not engraved, and there are 156 pages of the novel and 20 separate pages of notes by Lancelot, whereas the original contains 164 pages and no notes by Lancelot.

As charming are the illustrations made by Lefèvre for the "Lettres d'une Péruvienne," 1797, of Mme. de Graffigny, a descendant of Callot, who used his copperplates for kitchen pots; illustrations in this copy, which is on large vellum, are in the state of proofs and etchings. The illustrations made by Eisen, Cochin, Le Lorrain, and Vassé for "Della Natura Delle Cose," 1754, in covers by Padeloup; those made by Duplessi-Bertaux for "La Pucelle d'Orléans," 1780, and by Monnet, Marillier, Martini, and Moreau for "Romans et Contes," 1778, of Voltaire. The illustrations made by Marillier, his masterpiece, for "Fables Nouvelles," 1773, of Dorat, in covers of blue morocco lined with red morocco, by Trautz-Bauzonnet;

by Rigaud, Vispré, Choffart, and Eisen, the masterpiece of Eisen, for "Contes et Nouvelles en Vers," 1762, of La Fontaine, edition ordered and directed by the opulent Fermiers-Généraux of the kingdom; by Marillier for the "Idylles," 1775, of Berquin, in covers tooled and gilt by Derome; by Lefèvre for "Ollivier," 1798; by Leclerc for "Les Quatre Heures de la Toilette des Dames," 1779, with the original drawings of Leclerc for the frontispiece and the coat of arms; by Desforges, probably, for his autobiographical "Le Poète," 1799, with the original drawings; by Moreau for "Lettres à Emilie sur la Mythologie," 1809, proofs on vellum paper uncut, in covers by Bauzonnet; by Laffitte for "Point de Lendemain," 1812, on vellum, with the original drawing; proofs before letters, artist proofs, remarque proofs, etchings, fabulous states of plates, brilliant as diamonds in furious floods of light.

The "Liaisons Dangereuses," 1796, in two volumes that are favored by Paul Bourget with grade in a line with "Rouge et Noir" of Stendhal and the "Imitation of Christ," as volumes of profound psychology, have illustrations made by Monnet, Mlle. Gérard and Fragonard *fils*, in three states, uncut in pale-blue rococo covers lined with white, by Ruban; the "Amours du Chevalier de Faublas," 1798, four volumes, have illustrations in proofs, in etchings, and in colors by Demarne, Dutertre, Mlle. Gérard, Marillier, Monsiau, and Monnet; and the "Choix de Chansons" of Laborde, 1773, the mate of the "Contes" of the Fermiers-Généraux, in variety of costumes, a masterpiece of illustration in the first volume (illustrated by Moreau), a graceful, pleasant work of illustration in the last three volumes (illustrated by Le Bouteux, Le Barbier, and Saint-Quentin), has the portrait of Laborde ornamented with a lyre, which Masquelier engraved a year after the work was published. All the art of the eighteenth century is represented in this gift of a lyre to Laborde, this attribution of the symbol of the divine and immortal in man, made of clay but animated with celestial fire, to an uninspired, illyrical musician! The art of the eighteenth century gave its charm unreservedly.

It gave to the voices of the lovers, in the pastoral of Longus, murmurs of rivulets; to their lips blushes of roses; to their kisses the chastity of angels. In their eyes are their souls reflected, filled with Heaven. They are radiant with beauty and gracefulness, and guarded by their innocence, by their ignorance, by the calm and refreshing nature that surrounds them and that their happiness enchants. It took from the Farmers-General, and from the Governor of the Louvre, their fields, their forests, their vines and their prairies, and changed them into the satins, velvets, brocades, silver, and diamonds of incomparable engravings. It gave to the "Fables," wherein La Fontaine expressed Bonaventure Despériers, Louise Labé, Bidpay, Regnier, Rabelais, Hesiod, Guichardin, Tabarin, Grattelard, Phædrus, and Æsop, the inspiration, the science, and the elegance of the pictures of Oudry. It made Gallic the gods of Ovid; it represented the heroines of the "Contes" of La Fontaine in their triumphant youthfulness, the Constances and the Clities whom young men will ever applaud, dressed in gowns becoming:

> Corps piqué d'or, garnitures de prix,
> Ajustement de princesse et de reine.

ORIGINAL ILLUSTRATIONS.

It was not a painting of the Flemish school, a David Teniers, a Breughel of Hades, so enveloped with smoke as to make invisible the devil.

It is a manuscript gnawed by rats at the edges, in writing all enmeshed and of an ink blue and red.

"I suspect the author," said the bibliophile, "lived at the end of the reign of Louis XII., that King of paternal and abundant fame."

"Yes," he continued, with grave and meditative air, "yes, he was a clerk in the house of the Sires of Chateauvieux."

Then he turned the leaves of an immense folio entitled "Le Nobiliaire de France," wherein he found mentioned only the Sires of Chateauneuf.

"It does not matter," he said, a little confused. "Chateauneuf and Chateauvieux are one and the same castle. Anyhow, it is time to rechristen the Pont-Neuf."

This picture of an old-fashioned book-collector, made in an unknown masterpiece, the "Gaspard de la Nuit" of Aloÿs Bertrand, is composite.

It gives in an admirable synthesis the portrait and the state of mind of the collector of books antique; of the collector of books who, in doubt, assumed; of the collector of books who, when workmen failed in the art of gilding, praised as "chaste" gold lines lead-colored, edges of leaves livid, leather covers Jansenist; of the collector of books from whom books acquired nothing.

It forms an effective contrast with the picture of the book-lover, lover of art, lover of the beautiful, for whom painters who are great inventors and great colorists lavish cadmium, Veronese green, vermilion of China, all the colors of jewels, and the magic of sketches on the pages of books.

The book-lover is active, creative, powerful; and his distant relative, the book-collector described by Bertrand, passive, indifferent, flaccid. He orders, he pleads, he argues; he obtains the unobtainable. When he has obtained it the work may be spoiled, for there are great painters inefficient as illustrators of books; it may express the artist and not the writer; it may be a comment and not an illumination. He never yields; he never deceives himself with the illusion that Chateauvieux and Chateauneuf are interchangeable terms; he has the device of Eviradnus:

Without ever being absent or saying I am tired;

and if all human efforts fail, he may still charm books into perfection with passion in ecstasy.

In the library of Mr. de Forest there are two copies, illustrated, of "Mademoiselle de Maupin," 1836. One is by Edmond Morin, illustrator of "Monsieur, Madame et Bébé," of the "Chronique de Charles IX.," of the "Hôtel des Haricots," the walls in the cells of which were filled with sketches made by artists, prisoners of the National Guard in the time of Louis-Philippe; painter of street, garden, and park scenes, and unrevealed, except in this work, as an admirable interpreter, in lines and in colors, of Gautier. The other is by John Lewis Brown, celebrated as a painter of sporting and military scenes, and not in the least acclaimed as the diviner, the genial delineator, of the profound fantasy of Gautier, that this book proclaims. Every artist has, perhaps, a masterpiece unmade, a conception that only a book-lover might bring to light.

There are "L'Assommoir," 1877, illustrated by Edmond Morin, with pictures of Gervaise ironing while Lanthier reads, the fight in the lavatory, the parade of the newly wedded and their guests, the feast where the slang of Mes-Bottes excels, the dreary fall of snow—vivid, real, true as the text, and, as the text, prodigiously artistic; "Nana," 1880, illustrated by Jazet with a living Blanche d'Antigny, an acting Rouher, and the principal phases in the drama of a sad, bad life; "La Terre," 1887, illustrated by P. de Crouzat with a superb composition for a frontispiece of the sower, faithful to the text, and not in the slightest aspect reminiscent of Millet, and with scenes and personages of the Beauce, as Zola saw them, in the margins.

There are the "Chambre Bleue," 1872, "Composé et Ecrit par Prosper Mérimée, Fou de S. M. L'Impératrice," illustrated by Albert Lynch with figures that Mérimée, cynical only apparently, would applaud; "L'Adorée," 1887, illustrated by Jazet, bound by Stikeman in mosaic, framing a portrait on ivory of the Adorée in mosaic, valuable as an initial American attempt, for it is praiseworthy to attempt high art even if the result be not perfection.

There is "Madame Bovary," 1857, illustrated by Edmond Morin, with pictures of the terribly stubborn Normand villagers, the readings to Emma, the carriage wherein she enters at the door of the cathedral while the custode in uniform grumbles, of the scenes leading to the final desolation.

There is "L'Amour au XVIIIe Siècle," illustrated with pictures, vignettes, borders of pages, head- and tail-pieces, every one of which would adorn a favorite book of the eighteenth century. The work is by P. de Crouzat.

There are "Myosotis," 1838, illustrated in India ink on the margins, by Chauvet; "Fromont Jeune et Risler Aîné," 1874, by Dagnan-Bouveret, with pictures of the wedding festival at Véfour's, the workmen counting their wages at the cashier's window, the little paved courtyard before the mortuary-room, Planus and Risler in the concert-hall where Sidonie sings:

>Pauv' pitit Mam'zelle Zizi,
>C'est l'amou, l'amou qui tourne
>La tête à li.

It is because his work, in these illustrations made on the pages of a book, is for one person that the artist puts in it so much of his heart. Made to be engraved, to be exhibited in the Rue de Sèze, at the Salon or the Academy of Design, the artist's work is different. He knows that universal suffrage is incapable of conferring glory, that the public burns incense before idols that melt in sunlight, but it affects him often, as it affected Molière in the composition of the prologue to "Amphitryon."

There is the "Physiologie du Mariage," 1830, on Narcissus-colored paper, illustrated by Chauvet with pictures in India ink at the head and foot of every chapter,—graceful, delicate, subtle as Balzac; inspired and animated by his world of prototypes of d'Arthez bent on their books, of Nucingen inventing millions, of Marsay taming men by science and by charm, of Rastignac and Rubempré conquering civilization as invincible Attilas in white gloves, of Mesdames d'Espard and Maufrigneuse leaving behind them trails of light. There is the portrait, by Malpertuy, of the sensual, athletic, heroic, indefatigable creator of "La Comédie Humaine."

There are "Pastels," 1889, illustrated by Paul Destez with pictures in pastel of Gladys Harvey hesitating at the garden-gate of the man she loves, Mme. Bressuire at the tea-table, the Comtesse de Candale and her sister the Duchesse d'Arcole, the Señorita Rosario with her duenna at her balcony, Claire and Emile M . . ., Simone, the child at the fireplace in white gown and with hair like a vapor of gold; "Physiologie de l'Amour Moderne," 1890, with pictures in watercolors by Eugène Bourdin, tender, refined, subtle, intense, modern, and, as is the work of Paul Bourget, all powdered with dust of the wings of Psyche.

There is the "Miroir du Monde," 1888, with the engraved and the original illustrations of Paul Avril, that admirably reflect the aristocratic, original, independent, extremely sensitive ideas of Octave Uzanne. The book is bound by Ruban in claret-colored morocco, inlaid with a crescent of gold whereon Eros seated holds a mirror. The original idea of this symbol is Avril's, and it is painted by him on the white satin lining in colors of the region of stars and azure.

There are "Les Filles du Feu," 1888, with the original illustrations of the engravings by Emile Adan ; "La Pléiade," Curmer's copy on China paper, with original drawing in gold and colors on vellum by Feart for the frontispiece, original drawings by Ch. Jacque, Feart, and Jeanron for the ballads, tableaux, novels, and legends of the book, bound in blue morocco in compartments, with lining of gold cloth.

There is "Eureka," illustrated by Jules Adeline, whom the Gothic Rouen and the poetry of Poe inspire, with the picture in colors of Poe's cottage at Fordham.

There is that marvelous record of the vulgar, the commonplace, and the pitifully prosaic, "Scènes Populaires," 1830, with lithographs of the illustrations colored and signed in full, "Henry Monnier." Have you read it? Have you read the photographic chapter of it, "Le Roman Chez la Portière," wherein Monnier noted, as if condemned to the task for some horrible crime of his forefathers, the conversations of old women, all servants, in the room of a "concierge," of a "concierge" of the time of Louis-Philippe?

There is "Salammbô," 1863, illustrated by Louis Titz with pictures, bathed in antique, Oriental light, of the garden of Hamilcar where the mercenaries have their orgy; the lions crucified on the red hills; Salammbô praying on the terrace; the mantle of Tanit; the meeting of Hamilcar and his daughter at the steps of the palace; Salammbô and the serpent; Mathô and Salammbô; the sacrifice to Moloch; Spendius on the cross, a living helpless prey of the vultures; and Narr, Havas, and Salammbô dying. In the published correspondence of Gustave Flaubert one may read that he would not give the manuscript of his work to Michel Lévy for the reason that Michel Lévy proposed to publish it with illustrations. The great poet was one of those for whom real life is fiction, and who are in disguise when they are not wearing, as is their right, cloth of gold and jewels. Titz has magnificently illuminated his work. It is bound by De Samblancx in brown morocco, with small compartments in mosaic of serpents and pearls of the antique Kart-Khadasht, lined with green morocco, decorated with pearls and gold. De Samblancx has, in this work, obeyed the principles of the art of bookbinding so faithfully that, if the book-lovers were a grand mandarinate, he might be in it anybody that he wished to be, a prince, a baron in a fortress, a young page reclined on cushions at the feet of a blonde Yseult.

There is the reprint by De Vinne of the original edition of Sterne's "Sentimental Journey," illustrated with water-colors by Henriot.

There is "Mon Oncle Barbassou," illustrated by Paul Avril with additional pictures in water-colors.

There is a record of a Parisian theatrical season, entitled "Paris Théâtre," entirely in water-colors, and legends in the handwriting of Henriot. On the first page the final tableau of the first act unrolls its painted canvas and its gauze in the harsh clearness of the electric light on the stage; behind the scenes advance, superb in their clouds of muslin and tarlatan, in colors effaced, sulphur-yellow, pale-blue, pink of China, light lilac embroidered with silk, silver and jewels, the dancers of the ballet. In the scenes of carnival at the Opera there are dialogues worthy of Gavarni, as this:

— Vous ne voulez pas vous rafraîchir ?
— Si çà vous est égal j'aimerais mieux manger.

The Moulin Rouge yields a medallion of its queen, La Goulue, who has a pale, round face and the air of a lunar goddess; and sketches of the ladies of her court, Mâme Fromage, Mesdemoiselles Demi-Siphon, Nini Patte-en-l'air, and others not yet famous enough to dance with Valentin le Désossé, or to find their names in the open letters which Jules Lemaître sends by way of the newspapers to his country cousin.

The Porte Saint-Martin playhouse yields the scenes of "Cléopâtre," by Victorien Sardou; the Palais-Royal, of "Un Prix

Montyon," by Albin Valabrègue and Hennequin ; the Vaudeville, of "Le Député Leveau," by Jules Lemaître, and of "Madame Moncondin," by Blum and Toché ; the Variétés, of "Ma Cousine," by Henri Meilhac ; the Gymnase, of "Musotte," by Guy de Maupassant and Jacques Normand ; the Théâtre Français, of "Thermidor," by Victorien Sardou.

The pictures are accurate, the portraits of the players are good portraits, the costumes, actions, gestures, are faithfully represented, and the plots are admirably stated, although in a humorous and gently satirical vein. When Paris shall disappear like Thebes and Nineveh, when the Seine shall return to the bent reeds, when the names that designate the Parisian playhouses shall be effaced from the memory of men, "Paris Théâtre" of Henriot shall be a treasure of the archæologists. Forever it shall be beautiful.

"L'Amour à Travers les Ages," the title-page of which has the dedication : "A Monsieur George B. de Forest — Henriot, Paris, 1891," begins with the rape of the Sabines, illustrated by a Roman soldier lifting in his arms a woman, in costumes archæologically faultless, and the legend :

Ne permettrez-vous pas, ma belle demoiselle, qu'on vous donne la main jusqu'au Quartier Latin.

It pictures the lovers of the Middle Ages, when "le mari est à la croisade," of the Empire and Restoration in France, of Goethe's Germany, of Holland, where "on prend pour prétexte d'aller acheter une tulipe," and gives in chapters devoted to "La Chasse Féminine," "Menus Féminins d'Amour," and "Calendrier de l'Amour," as in the rest of the book, irreproachable works of art.

"Paris, Fin de Siècle," 1891, a similar album of pictures and legends by Henriot, gives aspects of the eternal drama in transitory scenes and expressions like this :

Alors c'est que tu n'as aucun amour-propre. A ta place je rougirais d'être la femme d'un mari trompé.

Henriot is an exquisite artist; he is, like Moreau, Lami, and Gavarni, a serious historian; often humorous, unlike Gavarni an optimist, he is ever poetical. He has the genius of book-illustration. "Bibliothèque d'un Bibliophile," 1887, is only a catalogue, although a catalogue of the Paillet library by Beraldi. It is only a catalogue, although the notes, by Beraldi, surprising, satirical, amusing, penetrating as sallies of Gavroche, may interest even those whom catalogues bore. With his illustrations in water-colors, in sepia, in oils, Henriot has made it an ideal modern bibliography. It unites science, art, wit, gaiety, enthusiasm, and irony; it is marvelously learned and marvelously comic. The book is bound by Ruban in brown morocco, inlaid with the book-plate of Paillet, a bookcase and the books, in mosaic of various colors, and lined with red morocco, inlaid with an open book of white vellum.

There are the "101ᵉ Régiment," 1860, illustrated with water-colors by De Sta, and "Le Drapeau," illustrated with water-colors by Bligny, in patriotic, emblematic bindings; the "Chansons Folles," illustrated with water-colors by Mès, and the love-poem of "Aucassin et Nicolete," 1887, so charmingly translated by Andrew Lang, illustrated with water-colors by Van Muyden. This is the large-paper copy of "Aucassin et Nicolete." The smaller paper copy is bound by Cobden-San-

TRANSLATION BY ANDREW LANG, LONDON, 1887.
BINDING AND DESIGN BY COBDEN-SANDERSON.

derson. His work is reproduced in "Four Private Libraries of New-York."

It is deplorable that Cobden-Sanderson is not a bookbinder of the decade, for he is the most artistic and, with the single exception of Roger Payne, the only handicraftsman with originality of all the artists in book-covers of England. But he does not deign to bind a book which he does not like; he has a style of decoration independent of the books to be decorated; he creates book-covers of Cobden-Sanderson. The art of bookbinding is an art of the book-lover.

There is "Au Maroc," 1889, edition of the "Société de Bibliophiles" of Lyons, illustrated by Louis Titz with pictures of the scenes and architecture ardently described by Pierre Loti, illustrated with an art strangely fascinating, and bound by De Samblancx in forms and colors Moresque.

There are frontispieces in water-colors, made by great artists, in many volumes; there are ancient missals and manuscripts with original illustrations; there are collections of caricatures, and military, clerical, and laical pictures, in albums and in works illustrating army records, manners, and customs; there are precious relics of ancient typography; famous classics; famous books of the nineteenth century; famous examples of art in book-covers — treasures that should be described here if it were not in the nature of all human works to be ever incomplete.

In their place imagine, not the dull uniformity which the indifferent call distinction, nor impersonal elegance, but stairways of ruby, arches of sapphire under which run rivers of melted gold, ladders of jade to skies of rock-crystal, and statues cut out of giant diamonds, holding in their transparent hands torches of pink light. For I have not a less charmed impression of the books with original illustrations, in bindings of the decade, made for the library of Mr. George Beach de Forest.

A BLUE DIAMOND.

THE Trianon of a book-lover, coquettish as the Queen's. A room the ceiling of which, in red morocco of the Levant, reproduces exactly the color, harmonious lines, and lyrical flight into azure of a wing of a book bound for Grolier. Tapestry of Beauvais; etchings of Rembrandt, Van Dyck, Visscher, Fortuny, and Lalanne; original drawings by Leloir, Du Maurier, Kate Greenaway, Blum, Chase, and Taylor; bookcases the crystal panes in the dark oak doors of which are lozenged; vases of the Palace; cabinets filled with jade, pouches, inros, netsukes, grimacing masks, figurines of ivory, delicate and complicated as if carved by a thin, epileptic tool; snuff-boxes, blue and white vases, jars, beakers, and bowls; ancient stuffs pale as petals of roses that have died of love. At the table, carved in massive oak, on a Persian carpet of silk, in a casket of lapis-lazuli, pell-mell with the rubies, diamonds, sapphires, and emeralds, the treasure of the reliquary, a book of poems not to be described, illuminated by cherished artists with fugitive rays of sunlight, flame of eyes, and blushing pink of lips.

At the table it may not be possible for everybody to rewrite Pindar, but it must be extremely difficult to write ordinary or common things, pleasantries against the bibliomaniacs, poetry, the Greeks and the gods, or conventional phrases of praise of books and art. There the imp of perverseness that tortured a personage of Poe, M. Prudhomme whose nose describes a quadrant, the pseudo-classics and the Philistines that annoyed Arnold, would have the air of masks at a carnival. The laws that they dictate to mountains would be sallies of clowns. Their thoughts, that by an antiphrasis are called ideas, about the art of forming a library would vanish as flibbertigibbets when the splendid Eos appears in her saffron-colored gown. For there are no books in the cases not ardently loved; none prized because scarce although ugly; none admitted because necessary to a set or indispensable to a system. They are beautiful, and they have not a double elsewhere. All converge to the blue diamond book of poems of the reliquary in beauty and art. It is not an accomplishment that may be lightly given as an example to others. It is like drawing the bow of Ulysses, a feat of Ulysses impossible to our frail arms. It was anticipated in print.

The Fortsas library was a parody of a library formed according to the art of the decade, anticipated and imagined by a book-lover in 1840, in the glorious period of the Romanticists. The Fortsas library had no existence except in the prophetic and disdainfully ironical mind of René Chalon, president of a club of bookmen at Mons. He compiled, with notes, a catalogue of fifty-two books unknown to everybody and unrecorded anywhere. Hoyos printed it and sent it to the book-collectors as the "Catalogue d'Une Très-Riche, mais Peu Nombreuse, Collection de Livres Provenant de la

ORIGINAL ILLUSTRATION BY VAN MUYDEN TO BRILLAT-SAVARIN'S
"PHYSIOLOGIE DU GOÛT."

Bibliothèque de Feu M. le Comte J. N. A. de Fortsas," to be sold by auction at Binche. On the day appointed for the sale the most learned collectors of England, France, and Belgium came to Binche with unlimited orders, found that the Fortsas library was a myth, and went back to their homes persuaded that they were victims of a hoax. Certainly they had been deceived. Baron de Reiffenberg, librarian of the Royal Library at Brussels, returned to the treasury money specially appropriated for the purchase of books of Fortsas. His own copy of the catalogue, one of the five copies printed on colored paper, is supplemented by the "Avis" delivered to anxious buyers at Binche, and by his report of the affair, entitled "Mystification Bibliographique," published on white and on yellow paper. Inserted is the following autograph letter of Willem :

Mon cher Confrère et ami :

Vous aurez déjà reçu, comme moi, le catalogue des livres délaissés par M. le Comte de Fortsas, dont la vente se fera à Binche le 10 août prochain. Il s'y trouve, page 11, No. 197, un recueil de quelques chansons flamandes imprimé à Londres en 1809 sous le titre de *Specimens of Early Flemish Songs of the XIVth Century*. Cet ouvrage est pour moi de la plus haute importance puisqu'il peut me servir à reconnaître quelques chants populaires que peut-être je ne possède pas moi-même et que M. Ellis a recueillis en Angleterre. Les planches de musique surtout sont pour moi d'un grand prix, aujourd'hui que je m'occupe de la publication très prochaine de mes anciennes chansons.

M. Rogier se trouvant à Gand ce matin, je lui ai fait sentir l'importance de ce recueil et cette excellence m'a répondu qu'il convient de l'acheter pour compte du Gouvernement.

Je vous écris en conséquence et vous demande à genoux d'acheter ce livre pour la bibliothèque, à tout prix, et de m'en donner communication aussitôt après l'acquisition. Je pense bien que je parviendrai à redresser les nombreuses méprises de son texte, soit avec les MSS. que je possède, soit au moyen devinatoire que je puiserai dans mes connaissances linguistiques.

M. Voisin ira à Binche; vous pourriez le charger de vos commissions, si vous n'aimez mieux les faire par vous même. Je crois qu'il convient de s'entendre avec lui sur les acquisitions en général. Je ne veux, pour sa part, que deux articles.

Si ces messieurs de la bibliothèque n'étaient pas d'avis d'acheter les *Specimens* À TOUT PRIX, ou même à ne pas les acheter à un prix très-élevé, je vous dirai que dans ce cas là j'y mettrai pour moi de 60 à 80 francs, et cependant je n'ai pas un trésor royal à ma disposition.

Je vous ai adressé Mynheer Siegenbuk. Sans doute qu'il est allé vous voir. Aurons-nous une séance de la Commission d'histoire au mois d'août? Veuillez me faire savoir vos intentions sur le volume d'Ellis et me croire.

Tout à vous,

WILLEM.

GAND, 20 Juillet, 1840.

Certainly they had been deceived; but Chalon very nearly explained the art of forming a library, the art of the decade, in the introduction to the fictitious catalogue:

Almost all the libraries formed during the past fifty years have been servilely traced on the "Bibliographie Instructive" of de Bure. It follows that the works represented by de Bure as rare, curious, sought for, disinterred, preserved by amateurs, are now to be found everywhere as fundamental pieces, and it has become true to say that in books there is nothing so common as rarities. . . . Count Fortsas admitted on his shelves only books unknown to bibliographers and cataloguers. . . . The

publication of the new researches of Brunet . . . made him
lose in one day a third of his beloved library.

The art of the decade, nearly explained by Chalon, is not
merely to collect books unknown to Brunet, or de Bure, or
Lowndes. It may make jewels of books that they lauded
and of those that they condemned. It is an art of the book-
lover, not of the bibliographer. Of course it would be easier
to depend entirely on the bibliographer, and not to form a
library of the decade, every book of which is a pearl of a
necklace the string of which may be broken without lessening
the value of the pearls.

A BOOK OF THACKERAY.

THERE are, in the original, inimitable cover of cloth designed by Mitchell, the "Airs from Arcady," 1884, that Bunner noted where the dryads and hamadryads dance; the "Paracelsus," 1835, of Browning; the "London Lyrics," Book Fellows' Club, vellum copy Number 1, of Locker, and his "Lyra Elegantiarum," 1867, suppressed "in consequence of Mr. John Forster's refusal to allow the poems by W. S. Landor, whose copyright he was possessed of, to be here published"; presentation copies of Dobson and Stedman; all the original editions of Swinburne, among which is the "Tristram of Lyonesse," 1882, containing a letter of the author to his publishers relative to errors in proof-sheets of the book; original editions of Thackeray with autograph letters and drawings, bound by Smith, Bradstreet's, Zaehnsdorf, Pratt, Matthews, Mansell, Tout, Bedford; "Bibliomania," 1842, of Dibdin, extra-illustrated with 148 portraits, nearly all proofs, among which is the portrait of Dibdin in canonicals, issued in only ten impressions; "Etching and Etchers," 1868, of Hamerton, containing this letter, written and signed by him:

When I was planning the book, a celebrated and experienced critic was so good as to give me some advice. His first general recommendation was not to write it at all, as it was sure to waste my time and the publisher's money. If, however, I did write it, I was to make the book very short and to be especially careful not to describe or criticize any plates particularly and individually, but was only to speak of the art in a very general way. I listened to all this advice, but did not follow it, and as the public has received the work with great favour, I can only congratulate myself on my obstinacy and unteachableness.

There are the "Cent Nouvelles Nouvelles" of Cologne, 1701, bound by Lortic, uncut, formerly owned by Paillet and by Desq; the "Madrigaux de M. D. L. S." (Monsieur de la Sablière), 1680; "Le Diable Boiteux," 1707, of Le Sage, bound by Trautz-Bauzonnet, frontispiece by Madeleine Hortemels, one of two proofs extant, formerly owned by Armand Bertin, Solar, John Delaware Lewis, and Eugène Paillet; "Les Caractères de Théophraste," 1688, of La Bruyère, bound by Trautz-Bauzonnet; "Les Métamorphoses," 1648, of the Platonician Apuleus, bound by Padeloup, formerly owned by Cigongne and Baron La Roche-La Carelle, the Baron a picturesque figure, in the world of books a stubborn classicist in whose view the art of bookbinding began with the men who worked for Grolier and came to an end with Trautz (but the Baron was blind for many months); "La Princesse de Montpensier," 1662, of Mme. de La Fayette, bound by Cuzin; the "Réflexions ou Sentences et Maximes Morales," 1665, of La Rochefoucauld, bound by Cuzin; "La Folle Journée," 1785, of Beaumarchais, extra-illustrated with portraits of the author by St. Aubin and Lalauze, bound by Reymann; the "Idylles," 1775, and "Romances," 1776, of Berquin, proofs of Marillier, bound by Thibaron-Joly; "Les Sauvages de l'Europe," 1760, of Louvel, bound with the arms of Mme. de Pompadour, presented to her with pretty verses inscribed on the fly-leaf by the author, No. 1974 of the catalogue of her books, and formerly owned by Mérard de St. Just and by Guilbert de Pixérécourt, "le Shakespeare des boulevards" . . . *rien que ça!* The "Etrennes de la Saint-Jean," 1742, by the Comte de Caylus, Crébillon the younger, and others, bound by Anguerrand, clasped in silver, one of two copies printed on vellum and formerly owned by Randon de Boisset, Gontrand, Gasc de Lalande, La Vallière, MacCarthy, Audenet, Baron Pichon, Potier, Quentin-Bauchart, and Noilly; the "Choix de Chansons," 1773, of Laborde, with the twenty-five proofs of Moreau, the lyre portrait, and bound by Chambolle-Duru; the "Fables," 1668, bound by Capé, and the "Contes," 1762 (bound at that period), of La Fontaine; "Les Baisers," 1770, of Dorat, the masterpiece of the eighteenth century, bound, uncut, by Capé. The "Daphnis et Chloe," 1731, bound in calf with compartments in mosaic, lined with red morocco, by Monnier; and the edition with plates engraved by Audran from designs of the Regent Philippe d'Orléans, 1745, bound in white morocco, lined with silk, by Padeloup, formerly owned by the Duchesse de Berry, mother of the Comte de Chambord, who would have been King of France, Henri V., if only he had wished. The prettiest vignettes, collected in albums, of the eighteenth century, which is the classic century of the pretty.

There are books of the Romanticists, plays of Augier and Dumas; the publications of Conquet, Jouaust, and Lemerre, as the "Œillets de Kerlaz," 1885, of Theuriet; the "Voyage Autour de Ma Chambre," 1877, of Xavier de Maistre; and the Musset, 1876–1877, in eleven volumes, on China paper, extra-illustrated with etchings of Henri Pille, Lalauze, and others, and with all the illustrations of Musset's works available. The publications of the Société des Amis des Livres —one of which, the "Aline," 1887, of Boufflers, is bound by Ruban with a veil of lace in gilt—and of the Bibliophiles Contemporains that Octave Uzanne directs; "L'Eventail," 1882, "L'Ombrelle," 1883, "Nos Amis les Livres," 1886,

and "La Reliure Moderne," 1887, of Uzanne. "Le Trèfle à Quatre Feuilles," of Georges Boyer, presented by the author, with an inscription on the fly-leaf, to Mlle. Suzanne Reichemberg, containing a letter of that charming sociétaire of the Comédie Française, and bound by De Samblancx-Weckesser in blue morocco, with mosaic of white, red, and green morocco studded with four-leaved clover.

There are the "Rommant de la Rose," 1529, printed by Galliot du Pré; a Book of Hours, not illuminated, printed by Pigouchet; another in manuscript of the fifteenth century, on vellum, with singular miniatures of great beauty; a "Recueil de Chants Royaux," in manuscript of the sixteenth century, with miniatures; a Persian manuscript of "Poems," 791 of the Hejira, of Hafiz; an "Office de la Vierge Marie," in manuscript of the seventeenth century, by the incomparable calligrapher to Louis XIV. and Louis XV., Nicolas Jarry, bound in one of the twenty-two mosaic bindings of Trautz, in blue morocco inlaid with white and pink dotted in the style of Le Gascon, lined with white, gilded with heads of angels at the corners, and the name of Marie in Roman letters in the center, in an aureole and stars; formerly owned by Eugène Paillet.

There is a little book of Thackeray which gives a title to this chapter because its salvation is due to the enviable qualities that have made possible the collection and mark it as the library of a book-lover. It is the "Horace" printed in 1719, by an imitator of Elzevir, a sextodecimo bound in old calf. It is marked on the first fly-leaf, in the handwriting of Thackeray, "E Libris W. M. Thackeray Carth. Dom. Alumni 1826"; on the last fly-leaf, in the same handwriting: "E Libris Gul. Thackeray. Carth. Dom. Alum. 9 Decemb. A. D.

1826"; and with the name of "Thackeray" on the title-page. It was Thackeray's "Horace," the "Elzevir Horace" mentioned in "Pendennis" and in "The Newcomes." It was found in the bookbinding shop of Matthews, where a famous, wise bookman had left it to be rebound! It is intact as a peasant would have kept it, for peasant and Cæsar are peers.

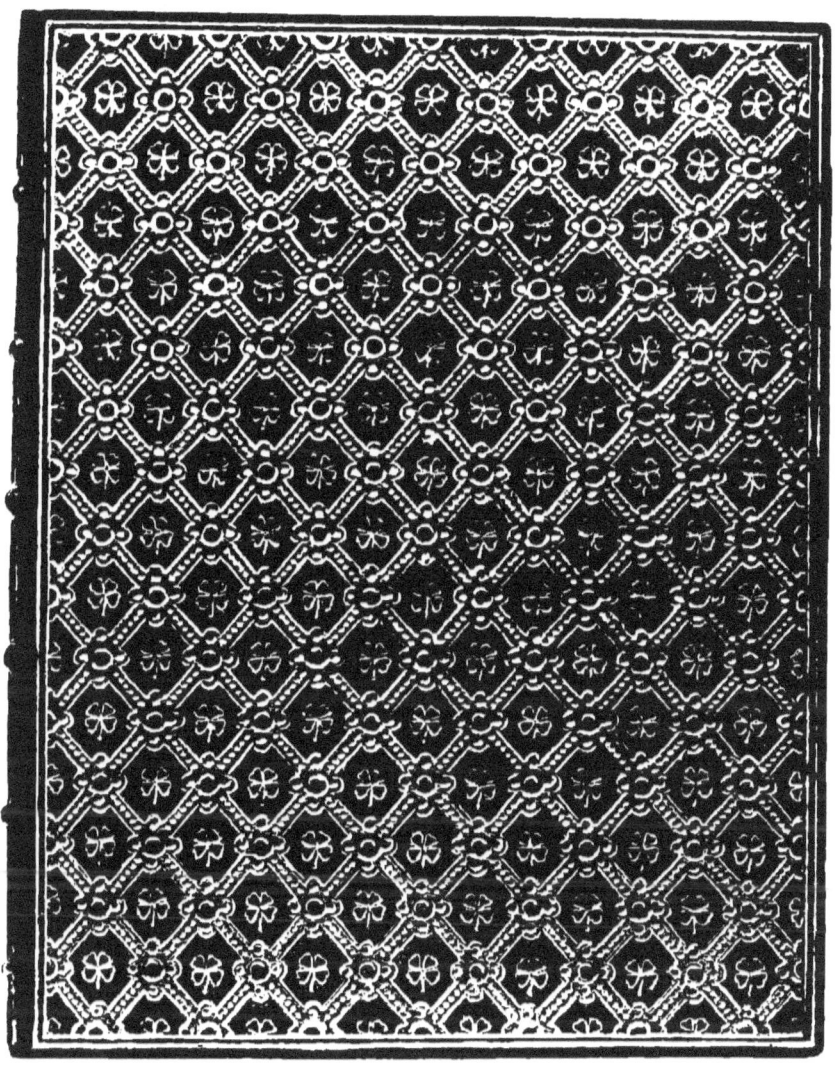
"LE TRÈFLE À QUATRE FEUILLES," GEORGES BOYER.
BINDING IN MOSAIC, BY DE SAMBLANCX-WECKESSER.

AN EPIC OF PIERROT.

In the time of the Romanticists, in the little playhouse of the Funambules, where the price of admission was four cents, the audience was a Chorus of Aristophanes. The players were, as in life, merchants, soldiers, pirates, bakers, peasants in crowds, through which passed, selfish as love, Harlequin and Columbine. Fairies recited to them lyrics of Banville; Cassandre, Leander, and Pantaloon ran after them, and Pierrot followed, indifferent, disdainful, sceptical, heeding nothing but to preserve, in his spotless clothes, and face colorless as the face of a god, the whiteness and glorious inutility of lilies.

Jean Gaspard Deburau then was Pierrot—a man of the people by his poverty, his irony, and his genius; an idol of the people by his gracefulness, his splendor, his refined simplicity, and the art with which he expressed without a sound the innumerable rhapsodies of his poems. Jules Janin wrote his biography; Gautier noted for him odes of the Olympus; Banville, Arène, and Champfleury composed for him heroic mimodramas. Pierrot was originally the Pedrolino—fat, greedy, and silly—of Italian mascarades; the art of France made him elegant, thoughtful, witty, more poetic than the Gilles of Watteau.

In the Carnivals of Columbines with small feet, Pulcinellos with sleeves of penguins, Tartaglia and his spectacles, doctors and druggists, Egyptians and Moors, Harlequins and Mezzetins, Scaramouches with mustache made of a straight line painted black, Titania and Ariel, Bottom and Caliban; in crowds blue, pink, violet, and iris; in tumults of satins, cries, cymbals, and guitars — Pierrot, agile, dumb, charming in dress of snow, appeared with gestures eloquent as songs of Orpheus.

A painter now is Pierrot; for the little playhouse of the Funambules is undone, the Carnival is subdued, and Geronimo has ceased to do honor to the festivals of life by attending them in a mask. In paintings Willette describes the frightful ocean of silks, satins, metals, wigs, scarfs, faces reddened by fever of pain and pleasure, that foams under the pale eyes of the moon, or sobs under the light of candelabra surrounded by clouds of white dust. Willette is Pierrot, pale as a phantom, inflexible as a King of Asia. In the marvelous autobiography of "Pauvre Pierrot," in pictures the original drawings of which are among the jewels that the blue diamond of the reliquary leads, he tells the pains of eternal exile, the sobs of lovers separated by death, the hopes that vanish into ether; he tells the sufferings of beings and things, thoughts captive in stones, lamentations of animals oppressed, and men a prey to misery, bent with hard labor while Winter covers the earth with its mantle and chills stars in the azure. As Barbey d'Aurevilly in novels, and Baudelaire and Verlaine in poems, Willette in pictures expresses the modern mind, the mind of the decade, sceptic and pietistic — a Gothic missal, the borders of which are in alternating dances of Macaber, and festivals of nymphs and satyrs. Pierrot, lover of the moon, poet, artist, Argonaut after Psyche, heads a long crowd, undulating as a serpent, of soldiers, judges, bankers counting their gold, grave-diggers, young men and women crowned with flowers, dancing, singing, voluptuous as priestesses of Venus, carrying the wax candles of communicants to an abyss. Willette, in pictures infinitely subtle and delicate, tells the epic of Pierrot.

The history of the nineteenth century is not perfect without Willette; it is in the marginal illustrations of great artists that the psychologists, the Stendhals, Taines, and Bourgets of the future, will find in books their clearest impressions of our state of mind. They may find of Bouchot's edition of the "Dames Galantes," 1882, this copy which has the original illustrations, that Boilvin has engraved, of Edouard de Beaumont; they may find of the edition of "Manon Lescaut," 1875, prefaced by Alexandre Dumas *fils,* this copy bound by Lortic, containing, beside the plates of Lefèvre, Hédouin, Lalauze, and Monzies, and a vignette by Marillier, drawings in sepia, pencil, pen-and-ink, and gouache by Dagnan-Bouveret for his friend Jacquemart; they may find of the "Chansons Populaires, Chansons Légères, Chansons de Salon," 1879, of Nadaud, this copy, bound by Ruban, containing the original illustrations in water-colors of Edmond Morin — masterpieces of literature, masterpieces of book-making, of designing, and of the art of the decade.

There are "Le Roi des Montagnes," 1888, with the original illustrations, that Mongin has engraved, of Charles Delort; "Les Fantaisies de Claudine," 1853, with original illustrations in water-colors of Paul Avril; "Vingt Contes Nouveaux," 1883, of François Coppée, with original illustrations of Henriot; "Fortunio," 1880, of Gautier, with proofs of Milius and Avril retouched with pencil and sepia; "Deux Mariages," 1883, of Halévy, with drawings and water-colors of Albert Lynch; "La Famille Cardinal," 1883, of Halévy, with original illustrations in pen-and-ink and water-colors of Emile Mas; "Jocelyn," 1885, with original illustrations of Besnard; "Carmen," 1884, of Mérimée, with original illustrations in pencil and water-colors by De Sta, and an admirable execution in the binding of a design by Avril; "Les Contes de Perrault," 1876, with the original drawings of the etchings of Lalauze.

There is "Un Bouquiniste Parisien, Le Père Lecureux," 1878, of Alexandre Piedagnel, with original illustrations of Paul Avril. In the time of the Romanticists there were Deveria, Célestin Nanteuil, and the Johannots; and Delacroix, who often sold, for forty francs to a model, panels and canvases. Alexandre Dumas refuses regularly every week 50,000 francs for a "Pieta" that Delacroix sold to him for 500 francs. But there are no original illustrations in books of Deveria, Nanteuil, Johannot, and Delacroix. The book-collectors of their time were not lovers of art unrecorded by de Bure. It was not in their view a valuable accomplishment, the collection of a hundred books inaccessible to others, and from which one might turn without surprise, as one does here, to miniatures of Hall, Guérin, Rousseau, Isabey, Gilbert Stuart, and Cosway.

Lydia of Horace need not talk in Latin, for the beautiful word CLARIOR is in her charmed voice. A book need not be in a particular language, nor of a particular subject, to be the book of a book-lover.

It must be as a poem is, ποίημα, a thing done, not one *to be* done; it must be perfect. If it lacks a line of text, a blank leaf, an illustration, it is a book in ruins. I know that, at a recent auction sale, a Mazarine Bible in ruins brought $14,800; but art is one thing and money is another. They are not relatives.

Of course a book-lover has money. Balzac takes care to provide his heroes with well-filled purses in order that they shall not be annoyed by absurd difficulties; but he never lets them acquire heroism by purchase.

Of one hundred books extended by the insertion of prints which were not made for them, ninety-nine are ruined; the hundredth book is no longer a book: it is a museum. Oh! the Waltons illustrated with colored plates of American governmental reports of fish commissions! The Nell Gwyns of Cunningham with the engraving that makes valuable Guillim's Heraldry! The Bibliomanias of Dibdin with queer etchings of poor, dear, forgotten Barry!

It was a singularly perverted idea of the art of forming a library, that idea of Grangerism, conceived at a time when there were no book-lovers!

The Pickering edition of Walton's "Angler," 1832-1836, two volumes octavo, enlarged to folio by Trent's inlaying of every page, extended to six volumes by the insertion of 339 portraits, 119 of which are proofs; 692 pictures, 276 of which are proofs; a drawing in sepia, two pen-and-ink drawings, twenty-three water-colors. . . .

And then, what? An imperfect book, built with the spoils of a thousand books; a crazy-quilt made of patches cut out of gowns of queens and scullions. Yet prints may be inserted in books.

A portrait illuminates the description of a man or the work of an author. There is in the book only one place for it: it is at the description or before the title-page. There is only one portrait available, the portrait of the man as described — not Napoleon in Egypt for Napoleon at Waterloo — or the portrait of the author at the age of his writing the book.

In the chapter of this book descriptive of books of the vignettists may be found examples of books *augmented*—in beauty, in interest, and in value — by the insertion of prints not made for them. There are none *extended*.

Do not *extend*. An ideal book for illustration with prints of its epoch is "Les Caractères" of La Bruyère. There is a personage to be discovered in every description. Every "Caractère" involves a portrait the print of which may be found. To find the personage, memoirs, anecdotes, gossip, letters of women, keys similar to the one published for Bussy-Rabutin's "Histoire Amoureuse des Gaules," must be consulted and verified. To find the print is easy comparatively — easy as Grangerism.

A fortune may be a positive force against the formation of a library. Having money, Louis-Philippe ordered his dinners at the caterer's; in the kitchens, extinguished and frozen, of the Tuileries chimerical nothingness was cooked in kettles filled with silence by vague domestics of solitude. Having money, Didot bought books prescribed by Brunet and Dibdin; on the parapets of the quays, under the sun, the books of the Romanticists were changing into dry leaves.

Do not fall into the error of those who, taking for a pretext the need of homogeneity, whereof Grangerism is the deadly enemy, say loudly that books should be bound in the country where they were published:

A French book bound in London! An English or American book bound in Paris! Horrible, most horrible!

This is nonsense. A book should be bound well, not geographically.

If the mind of a man be not pure, exalted, enthusiastic; if his heart be not filled with the immense love for beauty and humanity that poets have, he may collect books, he shall not form a library.

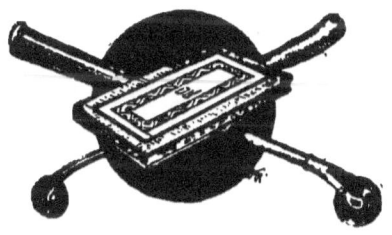

www.ingramcontent.com/pod-product-compliance
Lightning Source LLC
Chambersburg PA
CBHW030436190426
43202CB00036B/1358